A Quilt Is Meant To Keep You Warm

By M.J. Hobbs

Introduction:

Two things inspired these stories:

1. I started to ruminate about the 1980's when I submitted a story to a magazine and the publisher told me that "a gay man writing about the 1980's was sooooooo passé, Darling!" This coming from someone whose memory of the decade consisted of the walls of a crib.

2. About three years ago, when a friend of mine, a wonderful young man, was diagnosed with an HIV related illness, I started telling him stories about what it was like to come out in the 1980's to keep his spirits up. With his support, I started blogging my tales, and, 18,000 readers later, it has been an amazing and humbling trip.

Thank you.

Although the Age of AIDS was a scary time, it was also full of amazing people and funny adventures for a naïve farmboy such as myself. These stories are both hilarious and heartbreaking as a parade of everyone from nuns teaching safe sex to cops hitting on me at my grandmother's funeral make their appearance.

These are tales of memory so it is how I remember it. Others will remember differently. The narrative has also been streamlined in places to make the story and I have also changed some details to protect the privacy of others. There has also been the opportunity to clean up and expand this piece from the original blog postings and to correct some out of order stories, etc.

And, yes, I still write like I speak.

This story is dedicated to my Dad, for being the one constant in a changing world.

MJH

The Big Reveal

I will never be certain what compelled me to do it.

I was going to tell my Dad that I was gay.

Well, let's see. I was 23 and a year out of college. Carl Elliott, my first real boyfriend, and I had decided to move in together. I thought I was a big boy and I just wanted to be honest with Dad.

I asked Larry about it and he said, "Are you crazy?"

This was not the response that I expected to say the least.

"Don't your parents know?" I popped back.

"Micheal, I work in the THEATER! My parents would be surprised if I WASN'T gay. YOU work in a bank, for God's Sake!"

"I am not going to put it on my nameplate. Micheal Hobbs – Mortgage Broker and Big Fag!" I spread my hands wide.

"Believe me, boy, if your father had wanted to know, he would have asked you by now. He will ask you when he is ready to know. Until then, leave him his piece of mind."

"Larry, I can't do that. Carl and I are moving into a one-bedroom apartment. With ONE bed."

"That might be a bit awkward." he answered reluctantly.

"And Carl has many good qualities, but I would not exactly describe him as butch." I said.

"True." Larry answered with a slight smile. "But why now?"

"I have never knowingly lied to my Dad and never will.", I said.

"Just like when you told him about sneaking out to the bars when you were living at home?", he queried cattily.

"Hush...they never asked." I said uncomfortably.

"And they are not asking now!", said Larry.

"I am going to tell them. I just need to know how." I thought for a second. "How did you tell your parents?"

"I told them I got the lead in "Cabaret". That about said it all.", Larry sighed.

In the end, I wimped out.

I was off one Friday afternoon and stopped by the house. I will admit that I knew Dad was not home and that only my Stepmother, Rosemary, was. She was surprised.

"Micheal, what are you doing here? Is everything okay?" she asked.

"Oh, yeah. I just thought I would stop by for tea." I slowly said.

"Tea?"

"Yeah, just thought we could have some tea and talk?" I said as I filled the kettle and got out the cups.

Rosemary sat down at the table and folded her hands over her knees.

"So, what do we need to talk about?", she asked.

"Well," I said filling the cups, "I need to tell Dad something and I need to know how to do it."

"Oh, what?", she asked all innocent-like.

"I am gay and I need to know how to tell Dad?" I rushed out before I could stop myself.

"Oh, Micheal!" she trilled. "We've discussed it and he doesn't want to know."

That was certainly not the response I expected.

"What?!?" I sputtered back.

"Micheal, you Father and I discussed it quite some time ago and he just doesn't want to know." Rosemary answered.

My mind was completely blown. I sat there gasping like a fish while Rosemary watched me like I was going to explode.

Finally, a decision.

"Rosemary, I am going to tell him. I don't want to have to lie to him." I confessed.

We talked for a while but the best I could get out of her was, "Okay, I will tell you when it is a good day to tell you Father." I also gave her Carl's number as an emergency number and left.

AND THEN:

RIIIIINNNNNNG!!!!! Wha? RIIIIIIIIIIINNNG!!!!

CREEEEEAKKKK! went the bedsprings as we sat up in the bed.

RIIIIIIIIINNNNGG!!!!

"Who the fuc----?" said Carl as he reached for the phone.

CRREEEEEEEAK!!!

I stared at the clock through bleary eyes. It was exactly 8 AM. On a Saturday morning. Who would be calling-?

Carl was speaking into the phone.

"Hmmm?.....Yeah?....Who?....Yeah......Okay?" Then he turned to me with a look of sheer terror on his face. "It's for you?"

CREEEEAK!!! went the bedsprings as he handed me the phone.

"Hello?" I husked.

"Micheal?" It was my Father!

"Yeah, Dad?"

"Micheal....Would you and your" (beat - beat - beat) "*friend* like to come to dinner tonight?"

Carl, who was listening, shook his head in terror.

What else could I say?

"Sure, Dad. We'll be there. What time?"

"How about six?"

"Six?" Carl shook his head. "Sure. Six is good. We'll be there."

I hung up.

Time stopped.

Oh, fuck....

TICK...TICK..............TICK

The next 10 hours passed at the speed of tortoises having sex. About 3 P.M., I could swear the clock started to run backwards.

I was nervous, but Carl was completely freaked out.

"What if he greets me at the door with a shotgun?", he asked one moment. Then, "What if I throw up on them?", the next.

THAT was, unfortunately, a distinct possibility for both of us. I can't remember if either of us even ate lunch that day. Breakfast, too.

Both Carl and I spent the afternoon going through our limited post-college wardrobes and trying to figure out what to wear to appear non-threatening.

A pink shirt? Seriously?

No, you may not wear Grinch underwear in case your shirt creeps up and they show!

Bright colors were a definite no. Too gay!

No, Carl, those shoes look too fashion forward. We want my parents to think we are normal - well, nearly so.

I had to take three showers that afternoon because I had so much product in my hair that it looked unnatural. My hair can only be described as "limp" at the best of times, but that afternoon it looked like I had been struck by lightning. Finally, I covered my head with gel and put on a stocking cap until it dried. It worked but I looked like that kid on the cover of MAD Magazine.

After innumerable changes, we finally ended up dressed in black suits, white shirts and black ties. We looked like the gay Mafia going to a funeral.

Maybe we were.

SHOWTIME

Carl and I arrived at the stroke of 6 P.M.

The weather was definitely not cooperating. I was sure it was a sign of the Apocalypse as the heavens poured and lightning flashed as we pulled in.

As we ran to the door from the car, enough water got into my hair that I could feel it starting to move on its own.

So, there we are dressed for a funeral when my Dad opens the door. He and Rosemary are dressed in jeans and t shirts. Yeah, we were overdressed.

Dad took our coats and Carl and I sat on the couch. To be precise, we sat on each end of the couch. At each end of an enormous couch. As faaaaaaaaaaar apart as possible. We couldn't have touched if we tried. Non-threatening was the key.

That's when the questions began. My Dad started to ask Carl all the questions that you would ask the young man who wants to date your teenage daughter.

"So, Carl, what do you do for a career?"

"Where is your family from?"

And of course, the "Do you make a good living?"

I could have died and melted into those cushions right then and there.

Finally, my parents ran out of questions, and we just stared at each other.

The silence grew longer.

At that moment, a huge bolt of lightning crashed nearby, and my parents' dog came running in through the dog door. Dripping wet, covered in mud and scared like a rabbit and jumped...right into Carl's lap.

That broke the ice.

"I am so sorry." my Stepmother said grabbing the dog.

Carl was just covered in mud.

"Oh, my. Is that suit drip dry?" asked Rosemary.

By this time, we were all laughing.

That is how we all came to be eating dinner with me in a three-piece suit, Dad and Rosemary in jeans and t shirts... and Carl in my Dad's bathrobe.

An old photograph

There is a framed picture that I look at every so often. I supposed everyone has one like it. A group of friends grabbing a quick pic before running off to the next party or game or dance or bar.

I am way off to the right holding a sign from the gay pride parade. 1987.

Man, was I skinny. Huge Tom Selleck mustache on a too small face but I thought I was the bomb. Tank top and gym shorts and a hat with some forgotten bar name on it.

Lee has his arm around me. He is an extremely tanned man with an enormous drooping 'stache that hangs well past his jaw. The mustache is so long that it appears to have a life of its own.

He always mumbled while talking. I almost expected those handlebars to start interpreting everything he said for the masses like some sign language interpreter. And you would have needed it as he was a talker and a fast one. Always in motion, he was a mouse on Ritalin. Zip! Zip! Zip! I don't think I have ever met another person with that much energy.

Then, there is my cousin Kevin. Tall, wavy, chestnut hair. Captain of the swim team. Just plain beautiful and the first person I ever told I was gay.

If one phrase ever invoked Kevin, it is "always laughing". And, that is an infectious laugh guaranteed to make a stone smile. You couldn't help but feel that everything was going to turn out well when he started laughing.

If Kevin was tall, his boyfriend Ken was a mountain. A full head taller than Kevin, and broad as a steamship, he was also one of the furriest men ever to live. I swear that the hair started at the top of his shaggy head and did not stop until it reached the tips of his toes. Deep voiced and a big bushy beard when they were not the norm, his smile split his beard like the tide. Farm boy Ken was even wearing a flannel shirt and jeans on the hottest day of the year. He said they were just plain comfortable.

Oddly enough the next person to the left is my boyfriend Carl. I have no idea why he wasn't standing next to me, but it almost looks as if he is trying to hide behind Ken and the tree behind them. Big eyes and a look that says, "What on earth is a good Catholic boy like me doing here?" complete his portrait.

(low chuckle)

Next in line are Jose and Dan. Jose is Hispanic and standing there in a silver unitard one piece that goes from his ankles to his neck. He does not quite have the body to pull it off but who cares if he looks vaguely like a space alien from some '50s science fiction movie? Or he would except for the pompoms. Maybe "Forbidden Planet" meets "Priscilla Queen of the Desert"?

And then there is Jose's Dan. That was always how we described him. Middle aged, nice but nondescript, Dan liked to live in the shadow of his outgoing spouse. After 13 years of being together most people had even forgotten his last name so "Jose's Dan" it was.

There's Larry. The center of my social group. He was one of those people who simply makes the room light up by walking into it. Bespectacled and floppy hair with a theater trained voice that vibrated when he spoke.

Larry just wasn't talented. He was TALENTED. Give him two popsicle sticks and a ball of twine and a week later he would give you a sculpture that you would swear he had bought in a shop somewhere.

He could cook and clean and paint and write and act and sing and dance and, well, you name it.

I was so damn jealous.

And he was probably my best friend and I adored him. Everyone did. You just couldn't help it.

So, of course, he was in the middle of the picture.

Let's see, there's Mark, the banker. Always prim and proper. But he could be a very lascivious person when he wanted to be. I don't think I have ever met someone who was quite that "open" to new experiences. It was unnerving actually.

Oh, and, of course, he was terrified that the Bank would find out. But not just the Bank but his mother as well.

Some stereotypes never die.

There's Theodore. He was certainly a THEODORE. Never call him Ted. Never.

Recently divorced, Theodore was a diminutive actor whose personality far outstripped his 5'6" stature. His voice boomed and vibrated and made everyone take note. Big mustache and dark demeanor.

Theodore made his living voicing over commercials for everything from funeral homes to bowling alleys. And his voice did make every nerve in your body vibrate when he talked, and he damn well knew it. He was very popular in the bars.

There's Randy. Tall, effete, and overly politically active, he could not stand me. He thought I was flighty and immature.

And, he was right.

Finally, there are Al and Robert. They were the first stable, long term couple that I knew. Shockingly, for 1987, they considered themselves "married". Some whacked out Unitarian minister had performed the ceremony for them.

Al was a tall man in his late thirties who loved talking about his work. Tossed out of his home as a teenager when his family found him in bed with a neighbor, he had worked his way through college and his Master's and was now a consultant with the Federal Reserve. Tall and cadaverous, nothing made Al happier than talking about monetary policy. Despite that, he was a great guy.

Al's lover Robert was the polar opposite of him. Thin, athletic and supplied with an endless supply of nervous energy, he wanted to be an artist and was constantly painting and sketching. In addition, Robert was a black belt in karate.

Al and Robert were completely different but inseparable. Al's face would light up when Robert entered the room. Conversely, Robert never looked happier than when he was snuggled down under Al's arm.

Perfect is an overused word, but, they were, in actuality, perfect for each other.

There you have it: full noon and the cast of suspects are ready.

Smooth Criminal

I am a criminal.

A loathsome, dark hearted criminal.

To be exact, I am a blackmailer.

Let me explain:

In 1982, I was 19 and a sophomore in college. And scared. Oh, and gay. And I knew no one else who was gay.

Christmas that year was another disaster waiting to happen. Just before the holiday Mom disappeared along with her new Hell's Angel husband and my little sister and it was a choice between staying at college or being stranded at my Dad's house.

Hmmmmm. Cafeteria food and snow or being stranded with the family and no car in Ohio. I chose the lesser of two evils and stayed in Wisconsin.

Just kidding, of course I went to Ohio. God bless and love my stepmother for putting up with the moody and weird younger ass me. I was bored silly.

In an odd way, food poisoning was my ticket out.

I never knew what it was that I ate but there is no doubt that I got sick. VERY sick. Hugging the toilet about 2 AM sick.

After reexamining everything that I had eaten for the last ten days, I was completely ragged out. I could not have moved if I tried.

That is when I heard the phone ring. Thinking for a minute, I realized that it had to be my cousin Kevin's private line. He was living there while he went to Ohio State and his room was right next to the bathroom and away from everybody else.

I heard him answer the phone and start to talk. I really was not trying to listen in, but I couldn't have moved if I tried. It was all mumbling until...

"He took me home and we made love." WHAAAAAAAAAAATTTTT!!!

I couldn't help it after that. I listened to the entire rest of his conversation until by the time he was done, I was standing outside his door with my ear pressed against the door.

When he hung up, I took a deep breath and knocked.

"Come in?"

I entered and could tell that Kevin knew if anyone was knocking right then that they had heard him speaking on the phone. And he looked scared.

"Yeah, Micheal?"

"*KEVINIMGAYANDIKNOWYOURGAYANDIFYOUDON'TTAKEMEOUTTO THEBARSIAMGOINGTOTELLDAD!*" came out in rush.

What else could he say?

"Ooookay."

Pure Imagination

Does anyone remember the scene in "Willy Wonka and the Chocolate Factory" where he used a key to unlock the tiny door and the wall opened up into a room full of the anything you could imagine? I have had that moment. Instead of a candy factory, mine was called The Garage.

The road was dark and poorly lit and there were bums lying in the street every so often. A cat yowled somewhere, and you could feel the buildings watching you.

Stepping over a bum, we approached the building.

Imagine if you will, a tall, very attractive man with the build of a linebacker walking into a building as if he owned the place. Stylish, coiffed and perfect. And he knew it.

That was not me.

I was the gangly, oddly dressed boy following in his footsteps. Kevin's eyes had grown wide when he saw my idea of stylish. Bright red short sleeved shirt. Black chinos. Horn-rimmed glasses. Greasy mullet. Red shoes...and a black bow tie.

Clearing his throat as we left the car, he said "Just make sure you stick close."

The building itself was very scary. Nondescript, painted black. All of the windows are covered with plywood. No sign. The door even creaked as we entered.

In the hall, under a single fluorescent light stood the largest black man I have ever seen in a security uniform.

"I.D's", he growled. He looked me up and down and examined my license and then my face with a flashlight. Handing it back, he unlocked the door.

"Have fun, dearies!" he growled.

Just like in the movie, the door opened and color, light and music poured in.

I even remember the song that was playing. It was a heavy disco beat and Donna Summer's "I Feel Love".

There were men everywhere and all of them were eying Kevin as I was swept along in his wake. And the men just parted like the Queen Mary was coming through. I don't think any of them even saw me.

The front area of the Garage was what could be politely called a "fern bar". Lot and lots and lots of mirrors for inspecting every inch of yourself for flaws along with indirect lighting to hide all of the flaws you didn't have and wanted no one to see. Match that with all of the walls being painted black and the huge clouds of cigarette smoke and it is a wonder you could see anything at all. There again, all eyes were on Kevin anyway.

Trying to find a safe spot to park me, Kevin lead me to the dance floor area of the bar, and -

OH, MY GOD!

Men were dancing. TOGETHER!!!

I am surprised my eyes didn't fall as I watched them shake and twirl. I mean, I assumed they must have danced sometime - somewhere but I never thought in a million years that I would actually see men doing it.

To protect me, Kevin put me on a bar stool waaaaaaay in the back of the bar.

"Stay here and don't talk to anyone." he said as he looked me in the eyes and nodded to be sure I got the message that danger lurked in every corner. Clearly, I could pick up ptomaine just by looking at the wrong person.

I felt like a drowning man as he disappeared into the crowd in search of a beer.

The bar was loud and packed as "Obsession" by Animotion began to play. I even knew that song.

The place was filled with men of all shapes and sizes. Tall men, fat men, skinny men. Jewelry flashed in the night like stars twinkling. and every single damn one of them had a mustache.

Lights flashed and the music thumped as everyone moved to the beat. I was in Heaven!

Lots and lots of men wandered by and none of them in a red shirt and bow tie! I was just getting ready to slip it off and into my pocket when ---

A feather boa slipped around my neck and I felt myself being slowly turned around on the bar stool.

"Hi, I'm Jeffrey!" He most certainly was.

I don't know what was the more unsettling feature of Jeffrey. The blue glitter eyeshadow was what first caught my attention. The pink shirt with the crinoline ruff was a close second. Add to that the tight jeans and platform shoes to create a picture of true "manhood".

"I haven't seen you before. Are you new?" he lisped.

"Um...um...um" was all I could manage through the thick cloud of cologne he exuded.

"You look good enough to eat!" he said giggling and running his overly manicured fingertip down my arm.

"Erm!" I squeaked as the "fight or flight" response started to kick in. My mind automatically noted the exits were there, there and there!

"I bet you're fun." Jeffrey giggled.

Ten-Nine-Eight-Seven-

"How about we-" he purred as he leaned in.

Just as I was about to flee, a well-muscled arm slipped around my neck.

"Is this man bothering you?" injected Kevin.

And Jeffrey was GONE! I was saved.

"I can't take you anywhere." was all Kevin could say before he burst out laughing. Then I started laughing.

I could breathe again.

Later that night, after more beer than I had ever drunk in my life, we left.

A door had opened, and my life had changed.

I wonder what the bum thought when he woke up wrapped in a feather boa.

Dames, Dames Everywhere and Nary a Drop to Drink

I am not same person that I used to be.

I don't mean physically. We all change physically. I mean mentally.

To say I was an inhibited man is to be very mild. I was absolutely terrified of the world and everything in it. In fact, you may not like me after this story.

Spiders? Check.

Mice? Check.

Drag Queens? Check. Check. And, check.

Orange juice? Not really until the "incident".

Should I explain? Okay.

How many of you remember Anita Bryant? Former Miss America? Orange juice spokes lady? Enormous antigay bigot?

To refresh your memory, Anita Bryant was a gospel singer who found out that a county in Florida wanted to pass an antigay discrimination housing bill back in 1977, I think. "How dare those perverts ask to live in our towns and cities?" she asked. (Even though if I remember right she didn't live in Florida.)

That poor deluded woman then began to campaign against gay rights anywhere she could and sending sales of orange juice plummeting. Unfortunately, her efforts worked, and we are still trying to undo her "good works".

So, enough background.

I was attending my first gay pride parade ever in Madison, Wisconsin during college in 1983 and had decided to march in the parade. Anyone who wanted to could join. The only requirement was that you step into the parade and follow along after the last official group marched through.

I stood waiting with my heart pounding because I had seen the hundred or so protesters along the parade route when I and one of my frat brothers had walked up. It was a sight to say the least. Words absolutely fail me (and continue to every year) when describing some of the floats.

Finally, the last group appeared. It was an enormous group of drag queens all labeled "The Anita Bryant Brigade". Made up to look like the singer from Oklahoma, they all had huge fake teeth and black wigs. They looked like flight attendants gone bad.

I will never forget a very tall member of the group. He was at least 6'6" and in heels. Add to that the Miss America tiara he was wearing and he topped seven foot. He also had a sash on that said "Miss America 1946".

I was completely terrified.

So anyway, the drag queens passed, and I hesitated, took a deep breath, and stepped off the curb to follow them.

Right away, I was worried that there were cameras somewhere taking my picture and splashing my name on the evening news but, no, there weren't.

It was so liberating to walk down the street, but I had to be careful as I didn't want to get too close to those drag queens. I mean, it wasn't catching, was it?

Like, ick!

So, my friend and I were walking along when suddenly there was this shloosing noise and the crowd started to scream and run. It was like a bomb going off without the bomb.

Screaming homos ran by me and suddenly I was drenched from head to foot. Turning I saw a protester with a sign declaring "God Loves You!"

spraying me with a pump extinguisher full of what looked like...orange juice?

Not only had he gotten me but he had gotten the entire Anita Bryant Brigade - and they were not a happy bunch. The tall one screamed and launched himself at the guy and the rest followed. Howling like a mess of cats and twice as mad.

You could see the protester's face go from "Mwahahahaha!" to "Oh, shit!" in the blink of an eye. As he turned to run, "Miss America" landed on his back and the remainder followed suit. Those drag queens proceeded to beat the snot out of that man and no one in the crowd was going to stop them.

Finally, a cop broke through the crowd and rescued the protester. He went on and on about pressing charges. The cop finally said, "In my book you are lucky to still be alive. Don't you know not to piss off the queers?" and hauled him off.

As the crowd returned to normal, I realized that I was drenched to the skin and freezing. Without notice, I was surrounded by drag queens all trying to dry me off with Kleenex.

They were touching me. They were touching me! THEY WERE TOUCHING ME! ... and I was surrounded.

Before I knew it, I was sitting on a bar stool corralled by drag queens and being wiped down by "Miss America" with a bar towel.

I was completely petrified sitting there until one of them handed me a large glass and extended his hand.

"Hi, I'm Bill. And, you are..."

"Um, Mike?"

"Well, Um-Mike. Drink that down. You have had a scare. I want you to drink the whole thing."

I slammed the drink before realizing the whole glass was pure vodka. I started to sputter.

"That's okay, Honey." said Bill. "Get the anger out." He handed me another one.

"Keep drinking. You have a way to go to catch up with us."

It turns out Bill was a Wisconsin state trooper. His partner, Eddie, worked for the Governor's Office. And, "Miss America", Terry, was an assistant basketball coach at a local college.

The drinks kept flowing and as I got drunker, I also unwound. I even began to laugh at myself.

What a bigot I had been.

What an idiot.

What a moron.

By the time my frat brother was able to find me, I was ripped. The "girls" had been working on me for a bit and I was loose.

Waving goodbye, I got in the car. Looking in the mirror, I noticed the lip gloss and eye shadow I was newly sporting. I started humming.

"Bye, Bye, Miss American Pie..."

I Thought You Knew

This is not the chapter I intended on writing tonight.

This will not be my normal, hippy dippy, bunnies and butterflies writing style.

This is about what happens when a piece of news completely screws with what you thought you knew and changes a bit of the past.

Here goes...

So, I told my Dad that I was gay, and he was really good about it. Amazingly so, actually.

So, it was time to tell my Mother. Although our relationship was strained due to her extremely odd lifestyle, I thought that she would take it well. After all, she had a gay younger brother whom she adored.

My mother's younger brother Goog AKA Albert was the definite black sheep of the family. I still remember when he died of cancer in 1975 when I was 12. My mother took more than a year to recover.

Everyone says I look just like him.

Needless to say, she did not take the news well.

Flash forward to three days ago ---

I was sitting down with Dad talking about family matters. Somehow, the conversation turned to Mom.

"You know your Mom's brother was gay, right?"

"Yeah, Dad. Mom told me years ago."

"You know they never found his killer, right?'

WHAT?

"Dad, Uncle Goog died of cancer."

"No, Son. He was murdered."

"Mom told us he died of cancer."

"No, he was murdered down on the West Side. I thought you knew."

The Universe stopped and shifted a few inches to the right.

As he had died in 1975, I never really knew my Mother's favorite brother. I was 12 when he had died.

In a few words, my Father filled in a life I barely knew. Goog had been a brilliant seminarian destined for the Church. Something, probably his sexual awakening, had caused him to leave.

Seeking stability, he joined the Army and eventually rose to the rank of Captain. Again, he suddenly left the Army (and the family assumed it was because he was gay.)

Finally, he became an anesthesiologist and seemed on a path to success.

Then, his ghosts became too much to bear. Alcohol was the monkey on his back and he started to succumb. One day, he disappeared.

Months went by and finally Uncle Buzz found him in Atlanta. Living on the street and sick, he had reached bottom.

Uncle Buzz brought him back to live with him in his mansion in an upscale suburb of Columbus. I can only imagine what Aunt Winnie thought of that.

That is probably when I remember seeing him for the last time. Goog was a powerfully built man about 5'10 with a dark crew cut. He had a penetrating laugh and smoked like a fish.

He and my mother had the same eyes. Dark penetrating and changing color with your mood. I call them Charles Manson Eyes.

In other words, he looked almost exactly like me.

According to family, he was also a pathological liar. I assume that is how he hid the fact that he was gay from most of the family.

About six months later, I guess his mouth got him in trouble. He was found dead in the gutter outside a dive bar on the West Side.

My mother was never the same. That was the moment that marked the beginning of her slow decline.

The whole thing makes me wonder: When my mother checked out of my life, was it because she couldn't handle that I was gay or was it because she was afraid the same thing would happen to me? I have spent the years since her death detesting her for the void she left in my life.

She was a vile nasty piece of work but does this fact humanize or dehumanize her?

Did she actually deserve a second chance?

Enter Stage Right

You know when you meet your soul mate, right?

I mean the minute you meet them, the stars align. The birds sign. The butterflies chirp - or something like that.

Anyway, I was in my favorite bar, The Garage, and I was reading. I wasn't reading some trashy bar rag. I was reading a real book. To be precise, I was reading "Ender's Game" by Orson Scott Card and sitting on bar stool about 10 PM on a Friday night.

That geeky enough for you?

I like reading in the bars for several reasons. First, I had the social skills of an adolescent gibbon and really didn't know how to talk to people. This was a way of being around people and not having to actually talk to them.

Secondly, it was both the ultimate pickup gimmick as well as a surefire protection against bar trolls.

"Pardon me, but I have never seen someone read in a bar before." is how the conversation usually began. Perfect chance for me to look them over. If they appeared nice, I marked my spot and chatted them up.

"Have you read this?" would turn into a couple drinks and maybe even a roll in the hay.

If they appeared to be a complete and utter loser, it was the opposite tack. I would mumble something about preparing for class and slide my nose deeper in the book until they went away. It may have been rude, but it was kinder than telling them they were older than my Dad and smelled like mothballs, right?

So, 1985, I am sitting on this bar stool reading when I heard the question begin.

"What are you reading?" came over my shoulder in a baritone voice.

Turning, the first thing that I noticed were the eyes. Deep, brown and glowing. The noise from the bar faded into the background and I was mesmerized.

I was in LOVE. Harps started up. Rainbows. Rainbows. Rainbows.

"Is that book any good? I'm Larry, by the way."

Larry...has there ever been more beautiful name? Say it again...Larry.

I mumbled something and he sat down and began to talk. He was about my height and a little skinny.

I could tell immediately that our souls were touching.

We had so much in common. Larry, too, had a degree in theater but, whereas I was working in finance, he was working in a small children's theater and loving it.

As he chattered on, I fell more and more deeply in love.

I was so enthralled that I almost missed it.

"What?"

"I said, it is so nice to meet someone that I can relate to. We are going to be the best of friends."

Friends?

Shit.

Let's Talk About Sex

"We now observe the mid 1980's homosexual in his native environment. Among the ferns and mirrors, we find a wide variety of plumage..."

"Micheal, what are you doing?" said Larry coming up beside me.

"Playing 'National Geographic'" I said.

"Are you drunk, boy?" he asked while rolling his eyes.

"Not yet. But soon enough." Vodka number three was on its way!

"You have got to admit, Lar, that how these guys behave would make a good 'National Geographic Special'. Everything from those mustaches to the leather to those damn handkerchiefs hanging from their pockets."

To be brief, I was not a virgin when I went to college. The high school wrestling coach had seen to that a year before I graduated. That is why I always associate "The 1812 Overture" and cheap rum with orgasms and bad sex.

Tops, bottoms, versatile, bisexual, pansexual, omnisexual, leather, toys, bondage, frottage, puppy play, sadism, masochism, sado-masochism (of course) were all part of the nightly parade between the Garage and the

Eagle. With everyone sporting the same mustaches and haircuts, the only way to tell people apart was the Infamous Handkerchief Code.

What? You don't know the Handkerchief Code?

"What are you flagging?" was a frequent introductory question. It was an easy way to be able to tell whether you and the other person were into the same thing.

Simply put, if you wore the hanky in your left back pocket meant that you were the top. In other words, you liked to "Do Unto Others."

If you wore it in the right back pocket, it meant that you were the submissive. Or, "To receive was divine."

The code was very diverse, and you could get yourself into a lot of trouble if you didn't know it. For example:

"Lar, see that really cute guy at the end of the bar? I think he is looking this way."

"No," said Larry after looking around. "I don't think so."

"Why not? He is really hot."

"Micheal, I just don't think he is your type."

"Well, why not?"

Larry sighed.

"Do you see what is sticking in his back pocket?"

"Looks like a hanky. Maybe he has allergies."

"That would be a no. He has a brown hanky in his back pocket."

"What's so bad about that?"

"God, I forgot you are colorblind. Listen carefully, little man. Brown means he likes potty play."

"Potty play?"

"You really are naïve, boy. He likes scat! Poo! Shit!"

My stomach lurched.

"You have got to be kidding me. People actually get into that?"

"And he's flagging left which means he would be taking a dump on you."

"That's DISGUSTING!"

"We really need to do some education here, I see." smiled Larry. "Pick someone else out."

"How about that one in the blue jeans and leather vest. He's hot.

"Let's see. He is flagging green. You would definitely be his type - as long as you have $20."

"He's a hustler? Damn!"

Larry looked around like an eagle sighting a squirrel.

"Oh, stay away from the one in the leather by the back."

"What's wrong with that one?" I asked.

"To quote the yellow pages ad, he likes to let his fingers do the walking." said Larry.

"He's into massage?"

"Do you like having a sphincter that actually closes?" was the response.

"You mean he actually-"

"Shoves his hand up someone's ass? Yup" finished Larry.

I looked around in fear. Being colorblind really could get me into trouble!

Knowing he had had his fun, Larry smiled.

"Micheal, what's your favorite color?"

"Blue. I like blue." I answered.

"Good choice for an old farmboy. Just stick to blue for now and you will be fine."

"Why blue?"

"You'll find out soon enough. Now run along and tend to your sheep, Little Boy Blue."

For the curious, here is a link to the entire code: http://user.xmission.com/~trevin/hanky.html

The Villain of the Piece

I saw the first article you know.

It was my freshman year of college and I was working at the college library helping with the magazines and periodicals. I was reading some back issues of the New York Times because I liked the crossword puzzles.

It was only about three paragraphs.

Odd, isn't it? How something that small hidden way in the back pages of the New York Times could signal that the entire world was about to change.

July 3, 1981

"Rare Cancer Seen In 41 Homosexuals" was the title.

Kaposi's Sarcoma is a rare form of cancer that usually appears first as blue patches on the legs. The article went on to explain that there was no proof of contagion or transmission but that they were warning doctors who treated gay men to be on the lookout. It had been reported in both New York City and San Francisco and several of the patients had already died.

While I sat reading, my imagination started to get the better of me. My legs began to itch inside of my jeans and I dashed to the bathroom as soon as I got the chance. Sitting in a stall, I started the first of what would become months of self-examining my body.

Those restrooms were notorious for people having sex in them and what am I doing? Playing amateur dermatologist!

Was that a lump? No. A mole

How about that? A zit.

And so on, it would go.

Looking back, it is so hard to believe that the world was ever that naïve. Something so small sent the world completely out of kilter.

As time passed, more articles appeared. It was like a slow drip.

"More cases of rare cancer".

Drip.

"Pneumonia seen in KS Patients".

Drip.

"CD sees cases of rare cancer in Miami homosexuals".

Drip.

After each article, I would lock myself in my dorm room and take off all of my clothes. My roommate thought I was masturbating, but no. I was examining every inch of my body for blemishes and legions. Every mole became a suspect.

I almost died of hysteria when I developed ringworm. I was sure it was that terrible unknown disease.

Drip.

Drip.

Drip.

I confided in the College Health Center nurse and she was so blasé. "Honey, have you ever been to New York City or San Francisco?"

"No."

"Then you are fine, baby doll."

Even though I knew I shouldn't, I actually took solace from her assurances.

Drip.

Finally, they came up with a name.

AIDS.

And the flood began.

Who Are You? Who? Who? Who? Who?

"Micheal, what on earth is that?"

"What?" I asked looking around.

"That thing on your face." said Larry.

"You mean the mustache?"

"Is that what it is? I thought you were being attacked by a rabid caterpillar."

Larry and I were walking into the Gay Pride Festival in Columbus. Goodale Park was overflowing with more homos than I had ever thought to see in one place in my life. Floats lined up and everybody rushed around trying to find where they were supposed to line up.

During the 80's, dressing like someone famous was all the rage. Byronesque hair competed with leather jackets and sequins for attention.

My mustache (or attempt thereof) along with my white tank top and tight jeans was an attempt to emulate my favorite singer, Freddy Mercury, the lead singer from Queen.

I started belting out "We Are The Champions" at the top of my voice.

"Micheal," said Larry. "There is a huge difference between you and Freddy Mercury."

"Oh, what?"

"He can sing." quipped Larry.

"Very funny."

Looking around, thousands thronged and it was easy to categorize them.

There were the Michaels. How that many people found crappy leather jackets with buckles on them I would never know? And those single sequined gloves just looked plain stupid. Gay, white men trying to be a young black man (admittedly however weird) just did not make sense.

I really could believe him when he told Billie Jean the kid was not his son. Course, I could believe it of any of those queens trying to be him as well.

Of course the first one that tried to chat me up was a Bob!

"Hmphpgmh..." He mumbled.

"Excuse me?"

"Hey." He quietly mumbled. "Wanna see my 'Night Moves'?"

Ah! He was a Seger. You can always recognize them from the long hair and scruffy little beard. Imagine a mumbling seal in a wig and you have what was trying to chat me up.

"Tempting but no, thank you."

Mumbling something catty, the Seeger wandered away.

Pop Culture runneth over.

Leather Travoltas did their best to outcruise Cowboy Travoltas. Fake Urban Cowboys who had never been on a horse in their lives sauntered around while faux 50's bikers attempt to out-estrogen Olivia Newton-John.

A tall, beefy, Byronesque man was trying to chat up Larry.

"How did you get yours?"

"My what?"

"Your chin dimple. Genetics or surgery?" he purred.

"Oh, my. It's natural." said Larry with a smile.

Shaking his mane, the man continued to examine Larry's dimple.

"Every seen "Back to the Future"?" he asked.

Ah, he was a Huey! I should have recognized a Huey Lewis and the News addict the moment I saw the "I Want A New Drug!" T shirt. And here I thought he was advertising Alcoholics Anonymous Meetings.

Detaching himself, Larry and I wandered on.

"Look out!" said Larry as a crowd of self-tanning addicts stampeded through. "You almost got ran down by a herd of Wham-Hos."

"Don't they make Frisbees?"

"That's Wham-O." he chuckled.

I should have known from the huge, bleached smiles and the strains of "Wake Me Up Before You Go Go!" blasting from their cassette players.

"They think they are George Michael?"

"Delusional is more like it."

We wandered through the tree line.

"What is going on over there? It looks like a gang war." I said as I pointed to two groups circling each other like the Jets and Sharks in 'West Side Story'. Oddly, one group looked very punky while the other one resembled nothing so much as a flock of mutant cockatiels.

"Them? Oh, that's a gang of Maddys squaring off against some Kajs."

"Maddys? Kajs?"

Larry rolled his eyes.

"You really don't watch MTV much, do you?"

"I don't have cable." In truth, I couldn't afford it.

"Do you see the ones who look like they are wearing lace panties outside of their clothes?" he pointed.

"I really wish I didn't see men dressed like that but yes."

"They are all Madonna wanna-bes. Lucky Stars and Material Girls."

"That almost makes sense, but the others...?" I queried.

In point of fact, the other group, the Kajs, were the more disturbing of the two. I had never seen men in full body, silver Lycra before. Glitter competed with sequins for space on the bodysuits on men who really should never have been wearing something that tight.

Kajagoogoo was one of those one hit wonder bands who had the whole world humming their one big song but would be forgotten six months later.

And the hair! Long hair has never been my favorite, but this was really outlandish. Sides of their heads were shaved, and the other hairs were standing on end and cascading down their backs. They used so much hairspray that the ozone layer was thinning by the minute.

The two groups seemed to be competing for space at the front of the parade. I was expecting switchblades to appear at any time - or maybe curling wands as the two groups attempted to outpose each other.

The stalemate was finally broken when the Dykes on Bikes drove through and claimed the spot at the front of the Parade as their own.

Taking our spot, I finally gave Larry the once over. T shirt, jeans, bracelet and a silver chain.

"Okay, Larry. If I am a Freddy, who are you?

"Micheal, haven't you figured it out by now?" smiled Larry.

"What do you mean? Figured what out."

"Micheal, I am my own archetype."

And he smiled.

The Circus Is In Town

Looking back on it all and trying to remember how I felt and my intense naivete, it's a wonder I survived. Farmboy prejudices died a quick yet painful death.

Someone even asked me about it the other day. They wanted to know if all the prejudices I write about were how I felt then or if I still felt that way.

Hell, no, but if I didn't write about what I was like back then I wouldn't be being honest. Right?

We all change.

I hope I have...

Please?

Back to our previously scheduled program already in progress:

Larry and I crested a hill and the size of the parade and the festival began to sink in. It was HUGE!

Each year, I am sure the parade committee agonized over that year's theme but come on!

Over the years, I have seen quite a collection of the downright odd. There were the music themes inspired by MTV ("Vogue") and the pop culture references ("We Are The World"). Oddly named icons ("Holigays on Ice") and the almost appropriate ("Don't Stop Believing"). Disco themes repeating every few year and the downright terrible ("LesbiGay Holiday" anyone?").

That year's theme was "We Are Family". Oh, and we were. Blaring from every speaker.

The first group by tradition were the Dykes on Bikes. Literally.

I had always been taught to be a gentleman and I found it difficult to actually call them that. Yeah, they were a little butch, but I mean calling them "dykes" kinda of felt like I was giving in to the enemy.

Call me bad but I was raised to believe that women should shave their legs. And they were a bit furry elsewhere and this was years before I even heard the term "Brazilian".

The next group in line certainly knew how to shave their legs. And their chests. And their eyebrows.

The Ann Miller Brigade was a huge group of drag queens in majorette outfits, tiaras, and of course, flaming batons. The smiles were huge, and the hair was high.

Fast on their heels was the marching band. Light in their loafers and definitely out of the closet. I don't think I had ever seen that many trombones in one spot in my life.

Marching out of the park, a minor catastrophe almost derailed the party as a flaming baton misflew and wound up lodged in one of the tubas. Several handy margaritas and a huge blow succeeded in putting out the fire and putting the party back on track.

I quickly learned one rule about bar floats. They all look the same no matter what the name of the bar or the theme. Younger, shirtless gay men wearing huge smiles and a leather armband or two throwing beads and free drink coupons.

Next float. Lather. Rinse. Repeat.

I mean, seriously!

It was one thing for the float for the Garage to be full of twentyish gay men but some of the other bars were stretching it a bit. Didn't they want their own staff and patrons on board their own float?

The farthest stretch of the imagination along this was the float for the Toll House. Nice guys but the staff and patrons all tended to be age 60 and above. That was why we called it the "Troll House" after all.

Yet, here came their float. Hungover looking twenty somethings with more beads and beer cozies. Isn't there a law somewhere about truth in advertising?

Wonder of wonders, there was an honest to god politician walking down the street! Of course, it wasn't the mayor or anyone like that. I think it may have been the county clerk or along that line, but it really was a politician. We had hit the big time!

This photographer kept jumping around and taking pictures. He was kind of cute, but he almost got run over a few times. His flash was a little annoying and I wanted him to go away.

I must admit that the leather guys walking down the street were kind of hot. Well, some of them that is. Let's face it, Tom Selleck in leather would turn just about anyone on. So, the hot ones were very hot. Row after row of hot men in black leather vests and pants with sunglasses definitely made the atmosphere very steamy.

But then...

Some of them boys just needed to put their clothes back on. Assless chaps are great IF YOU HAVE AN ASS. They are not made to hang loose, and they certainly aren't made in Grande size.

To quote that old song "The Streak", Ethel put your clothes back on.

Please.

The little photographer annoyed one of the leather guys by taking so many flash pictures that he got bitch slapped with a big black dildo.

The best part of the parade had to be the protesters.

Toothless wonders competed with Bible thumping pastors in a cacophony of reasons as to why I would be burning in hell for all eternity. Several spectators were trying to argue with them.

My favorite was a guy with a sign with an arrow that said "Yeah, I fucked him. I've had better." who insisted on standing next to the really cute bible thumper. Once the pastor realized what his sign said, he tried to take it away from him and tug of war ensued. All that resulted from this was a bloody nose for the minister and a photograph on the cover of the local paper with him holding a ripped sign that said "fuck".

The little photographer was in hog heaven. I just wanted him to go away but he finally turned to me and said, "Hi, I'm Carl."

Eyes always do it to me. The next thing I knew, I was walking down the street holding hands with him. Seriously, I WAS HOLDING HANDS with a guy.

We wandered through the festival like innocents abroad.

That was when he said those fateful words.

"Are you busy tomorrow night?"

The Date From Hell

The coins dropped into the payphone and I dialed.

He answered on the first ring.

"Hello?"

"Micheal?"

"Yeah, Larry. I need your help."

"Micheal, do you have any idea what time it is?" he yawned.

"About 3 A.M."

"Are you drunk?"

"I can only wish. Anyway, I will explain when you get here." I gave him the address.

"This had better be good." he warned hanging up.

"That depends on your point of view", I mumbled as I stepped over a firehose and sat down on the curb to wait.

****

Our date had started off innocently enough.

I had bought my first car from Dad, a Datsun B-210, and I was so proud of it. It was older and a little beat up and I loved it.

Carl did not have a car, so I picked him up at his place and we headed down to German Village to eat. The Olde Mohawk Tavern allowed us a chance to eat and to talk and to get to know each other better.

Turns out Carl was a graphics designer at a small advertising agency. He also loved photography and contributed to a local gay publication called Gay Times!

Everything was going swimmingly until, "and that's when we got engaged."

Say, what?

"Mary and I got engaged after I graduated college."

"You're straight?"

"Oh, no. Bisexual is the right term."

"Does that even exist?" I asked quizzingly.

"More than you know. I told her I wanted to date guys and she agreed"

"Isn't that a bit odd?"

"Oh, not at all. As a matter of fact, you can meet her sometime if you like." he offered.

Luckily, the waiter showed up just then to take our order.

To call our waiter stereotypical is to insult gay waiters everywhere. And he was 80's-ed out. A satin silver shirt complimented with gold chains immediately caught the eye. Add to that a faux bleached blond Mohawk that cascaded down his back and a pencil goatee and the picture was almost complete.

I don't see how he could even move as his pants were so tight.

"Can I get you boys an appetizer?" he suggested while shaking his locks.

"Sure. How about the bruschetta?" I asked.

"Got it." he said vaguely and wandered off.

"So, does Mary live around here?" I queried Carl half afraid some unidentified woman would pop up suddenly.

"Yes, she lives on the North Side."

"And how did you break the news to her that -"

"Sorry, boys, but we are out of bruschetta. Did you want something else?" interrupted the waiter.

"Just bring us the cheese dip." I snapped.

The waiter floated away.

"I just told her that I needed to find myself. She understood." Carl answered.

"I am not certain that I consider sleeping with guys finding -"

"Are you boys ready to order?" interrupted the waiter yet again and raising my anxiety level further.

"Just get me a vodka please." I growled.

Carl eyed me oddly.

"It really is all right." he said.

"Okay," I sighed. "Let's get back to our date. Did you want to go to -" I began.

"Here you are. One vodka." interrupted the waiter again. "Did you want to hear the specials?"

"No thanks. Please just bring me a steak with fries."

Carl quickly ordered, and the waiter left.

"How about we hit the Book Loft after this?" Carl asked.

A book store? Cool! I could feel our date starting to get back on track -

"I am so sorry, Hon, but I forgot to ask how you wanted that steak fixed." inserted the waiter.

"Just well done, please." I popped.

Huffy, the waiter wandered off.

Carefully, Carl explained about Mary and honestly, she sounded like a lovely person. I just didn't know how I felt getting involved with someone who couldn't commit 100%. Ah, well, life is full of compromises.

By this time, it was getting later and after we finished dinner, we took a walk to the bookstore. Finding it closed (it was 10 p.m. after all) we took a long walk through Schiller Park back to my car.

Not wanting the evening to end so quickly, I suggested that we head to the Garage for a drink and off we went.

As you can imagine on a Saturday night, the bar was hopping. Loud music and louder people poured onto the sidewalk as we entered.

Grabbing us a couple of beers and parking Carl at a table, I hit the restroom. That is when the weirdo spotted me.

"Hey, Dude. I'm Matt." came over the urinal stall wall followed by a hand trying to shake mine.

I am pee shy at the best of times but this took the cake. Trying my best to ignore him, I finished up and washed. That is when I found Matt blocking the door.

"Hey, Dude. I'm Matt." he said again extending his hand.

"Nice to meet you." I said shaking his hand and trying to get by him.

"You know you are kind of cute." Matt said blocking the door with his foot.

"Thanks," I said accidentally stomping on his foot.

"Oh, I am sorry." I threw over my shoulder as I rushed through the door.

That is when I found Carl at the table being monopolized by a figure in white and silver satin. Our waiter. If he had flashed before, now he had all the subtle showmanship of a cockatoo.

And he was very, very drunk.

And he was trying to pick up my date.

As I forced my way between the cockatoo and my date, he shook his sandalwood scented locks and said, "Hey man, I was talking here."

"Look we are on a date. Go away!"

"But-"

That is when my bar stool hit him in the crotch as I pulled it back to sit down.

"Oh, I'm sorry." I said as he wheezed away.

Sitting down, Carl and I started to chat, and it finally seemed as though our date was starting to slide along.

It turns out the monthly gay paper that Carl what worked for was looking for writers. I am no Hemingway by any means, but I have always enjoyed reading and it seemed something I can help with.

As we spoke, we started to lean into each other. I thought "Oh, my God. He is going to kiss me!"

That is when I caught sight of an odd look on Carl's face. He was staring at something over my shoulder.

Turning - Yup! It was the waiter. He was leaning against the bar and staring a hole through Carl's left shoulder. Preening like the cockatoo he was, he was shaking his locks and trying to throw what I suppose was meant to be a smoldering look at my date.

Throwing back another shot, the waiter winked at Carl and sniffed at me.

Sliding my bar stool to change Carl's line of sight, we started to talk again. Turns out that Gay Times! needed someone to report on the Arts and Hey! I have a degree in Theater! Seemed like a natural match.

Carl started to lean in again and I could feel the kiss coming. The conversation was running fast when I glanced up and saw him.

Matt, the men's room weirdo. Posing against the bar and working his black mullet for all that it was worth. And staring over my date's shoulder at me.

Carl must have seen the look on my face because he turned and said, "Do you know him?"
"No, and I really don't want to."
Smiling, Carl moved his bar stool to move the bathroom mutant out of my view. Our conversation started again. Carl was wearing Old Spice and smelled good. He smiled at me and started to move in when his eyes went wide.
Knowing without even having to turn around, but of course I did, the cockatoo had shifted his spot on the bar so that he was back in a straight-line view to Carl. I suppose the pose was meant to be seductive but when

one can barely stand it is more of a full body jiggle to remain upright than Mae West.

Shifting again, Carl and I kept talking about our hobbies and what we wanted out of life. Finally, he leaned in and -

The bathroom mutant had shifted his place again and his eyes were boring a hole in my forehead.

Shift. Talk. Waiter. Shift. Talk. Mutant. The merry-go-round continued for about an hour.

I never got the kiss.

At last, Carl said, "Listen, the bar is closing in a few. How about if we hit the IHOP on North High for a snack?" Breakfast at the International House of Pancakes was an after-bar tradition in Columbus.

Leaving the beer I had been nursing all night, we hopped in my car and headed off north to campus on High Street. Chattering away as we drove, I found out that Carl had grown up in the next town over from me. We were even the same age. Small world.

As we passed Hudson Street, I noticed a car parked in my lane. It was a very busy section of High Street so I stopped the car to allow traffic to die down so I could pass. It was going to be a while, so I put the car in PARK. Taking advantage of the pause, Carl leaned in to finally give me that kiss I had been hoping for all night. And it was good. Really good.

And, then--

I guess it was just fate that made me glance briefly in the rear-view mirror. That is when I saw the car coming up behind me in my lane. Very fast and he was not stopping.

Pushing Carl back into his seat, I yelled, "HOLD ON!"

CRASH!!! BOOM!!! SCRAPE!!! SMASH!!!

The speeding car plowed into us without even braking. My little car didn't stand a chance as it was crushed into the parked car ahead of us. The frame bowed upward, and we were pressed against the ceiling. Smoke began to seep out from under the dashboard.

Turning to Carl, I shouted, "GET OUT NOW!"

This did not prove to be an obstacle as the side windows had shattered. We basically flopped out on the pavement like fish. I only had a few cuts and bruises.

I started towards the car that had hit me and that it when it peeled off in a cloud of smoke and leaking fluids.

"COME BACK HERE, YOU GODDAMN SONOFABITCH!" I screamed.

Stumbling around the car, I found Carl lying on the sidewalk.

"Are you okay?" I asked as I tried to search him for broken bones, popped eyeballs, that sort of thing.

"My back hurts and I am really dizzy..." he moaned.

A car pulled up and the window slid down.

"What happened?" asked Matt, the bathroom weirdo.

"A white Mustang plowed into us!"

"Shit!" he mumbled and was gone!

A crowd had begun to gather.

"Someone, please call the cops." I pleaded as I went to check on Carl.

I don't know how long it was, but the cops were suddenly right there. Two of them. They parked in front of the smashed parked car and came up to me.

"So why did you hit that car?" demanded the older cop.

Astounded and stressed, I was not taking any shit.

"Have you seen the back of my car? I was pushed into it."

Humphing and not really wanting to believe it, he swung around the back of my car only to discover that I was right.

"Are you sure you haven't been drinking?" he queried hopefully.

"Sir, I have had half a beer in the last three hours and will gladly take a sobriety test. I was stopped when I was slammed into by another car."

The cop seemed crestfallen, but he started to record all of the details. He perked up when he found that the license plate from the white car had fallen off and was lying in the street. A clue!

I walked back over to check on my date and found the younger cop talking to him. It did not seem like normal questions. In fact, he was hitting on Carl.

What the hell?

"Is there an ambulance on its way? He says his back is hurt."

"Oh, okay..." and he got on the radio.

About this time, the white Mustang came back followed by another car and parked right behind me. Leaking fluids and steam, it was obviously about to fall apart. Clearly drunk, the driver stepped out of the car.

It was the waiter.

"I told him he had to come back or they would charge him with leaving the scene." Even better, it was Matt, the bathroom mutant.

"Yeah, we were heading to IHOP when he got a bit ahead of me. I found him at the gas station up the way and made him come back."

"Thanks."

By this time, the ambulance had arrived and the EMT's were checking Carl over. No broken bones. Great! Bumps and bruises galore. Not so great but okay. Sprained back. Probably.

"So, what are you up to tomorrow night?" asked the men's room weirdo.

"Are you fucking kidding me?" Go the goddamn hell away!" I snapped.

He backed off.

Using all of his detective powers, the older cop noticed something amiss with the cockatoo driving the white car. The sobriety test would have been amusing if I wasn't so agitated. Instead of touching his nose, he touched his ear. And, there are not three "M's" in your ABC's.

The sobriety walk ending in three falls was worthy of Jerry Lewis. Giving up any pretense, the waiter finally sat down on the curb to await his fate. At the ambulance, the crew was finally ready to take Carl to the hospital. Mary was going to meet him there and make sure he got home.

As they wheeled him off, he quipped, "How about tomorrow night we stay in?".

The older cop was taking pictures and filing reports.

The younger cop and Matt were now engrossed in conversation and walking towards Matt's car.

All was going better until the waiter decided that he needed a cigarette. Normally, the only victim would have been his health, but he was not in an optimum spot for smoking. Sitting on a curb while all kinds of liquids drip from three wrecked cars nearby and ran into the gutter.

And between his feet.

The first sign of trouble was when the little man started screaming and flailing on the sidewalk as his shoes caught fire. The cops ran towards him and managed to get him put out before he really hurt himself but flames slowly crept towards the leaking Mustang.

The crowd ran to get out of danger.

So, that is how the fire truck arrived. A few extinguishers and a couple of fire hoses got the situation under control. Luckily, my car never caught fire but that didn't matter as it would never drive again.

An ambulance bundled the drunken waiter to the emergency room while Matt the weirdo was handcuffed and taken off by the older cop after finding a bag of leafy green stuff on the front seat of his car.

The younger cop stayed with me while the three tow trucks carried off my car, the white Mustang and the car I had been pushed into. The cops had been unable to find the owner.

Just before he drove off, the young cop leaned out the window and handed me a piece of paper.

"Call me sometime," he said and drove off.

It was his home phone number.

That is when it started to rain.

****

"So, Larry. That's it."

Raising one eyebrow, "Well, Micheal, you certainly know how to have a good time." he said.

Yeah, I know how to have a good time all right.

The God of Sex

It was a lazy Sunday night when I first met him.

I was sitting in the Garage talking to my cousin Kevin and his boyfriend Ken. My friend Mark, the banker, and I had joined them for a drink. It had been a slow weekend and we were all having that final drinking session before work the next day when all talk stopped.

Even the music stopped. Or so it seemed.

Kevin's face went blank and his eyes widened. Not knowing what was happening I turned and...

Pure Sex had arrived.

How best to describe him? Middle height. Short black hair. Mustache. Half Italian - Half Irish. 100% sex.

Words simply fail to conduct how incredibly sensuous this man was. Take the masculinity of Tom Selleck and add the overwhelming sensuality of Bo Derek and then double it and you had this man.

Everyone in that bar immediately wanted him. Man. Woman. Fern. Straight. Gay. It didn't matter. The man could make jello horny.

He turned in a practiced move and the entire bar started up again.

"Who is that?" I whispered to Kevin.

"I'm not sure. I think he used to be a Colt model." Colt was the gold standard for gay porn in the '80's.

"Really? Wow!"

I watched him as he walked across the room. Every single movement seemed to flow in such a way as to accentuate his total dominance of the room. A flick of the head. A half smile. Even the way he grabbed his wallet from his back pocket outlined how he filled out his jeans.

"I hear his lover is some closeted company president." said Mark.

"I heard he was a former Navy Seal" said Ken.

The rumors flew hot and heavy around the table as the mystery man made his way around the bar. He was with a tall, handsome black man who was clearly just a friend. The rumored CEO must have stayed in for the night.

Our conversation had begun to drift back to more normal topics like how dull our jobs were, etc., when -

"Pardon me, can I borrow this stool?" came over my shoulder.

Turning, It Was Him!

If he had exuded sex from clear across the room, it was twice as overpowering now. Half smile. Oxford button down shirt open just enough to see chest hair. Tight abs showing and jeans so tight he had to have been poured into them.

"Hmmmmmm?" was all I could muster.

"Can I borrow this stool?" he asked again while signaling to the next table where his friends were sitting.

I could only nod.

"Thanks."

"Nghhh..."

He smiled. "Kid, shut your mouth. You're drooling." and turned away.

"Tracy, leave that poor boy alone." laughed his friend.

Smiling, he sat down with his companions.

Shaking my head to break the spell, I tried to reenter the conversation but was clearly distracted.

The God of Sex had spoken to me. Me, personally!

The evening moved along but I couldn't help but watch the man - Tracy, they had called him. Every gesture. Every movement. Even every facial expression seemed perfectly designed to make you desire him.

I was beyond overwhelmed. I could barely say hello to someone without completely embarrassing myself and here was someone who didn't have to speak a word to control an entire room full of people.

Such confidence. I was both turned on and jealous beyond words.

I must have been staring a little too long because I saw one of Tracy's friend nudge him and nod at me.

"I think you have a new puppy, Tracy."

Those green eyes turned to stare at me and he purred, "Hey, Kid. I'm Tracy. Nice to meet you."

"I'm, um, Mike." I stammered out somehow. He winked, and my heart skipped a beat.

"Take care for now." And he and his friends glided to the back of the bar.

As they went off, I heard one go "Tracy Anders, you are a cruel, cruel man."

Feeling flushed, and excited, I didn't know what to do. Oh, and I was turned on like a light bulb. 100 watts!

As life began to flow again, I realized that I had to go to the bathroom quite badly. I detest public bathrooms and I had to really be needing to go if I was doing so in public. I found my way to restroom and sat in a stall.

After a few minutes, I was ready to leave when someone else entered the restroom. As they didn't go to the urinal or enter a stall, I could only assume they were doing cocaine off the sink with the mirror. Not wanting to interrupt their partaking, I waited and waited.

Oddly, it didn't seem like they were doing coke. In fact, they were whispering to themselves.

"What if I stood this way instead?"

"Should I unbutton a couple more?"

"I have to look damn fine tonight. I must!"

"Girl, you look amazing!"

Peeking out through the door of the stall I saw that it was Tracy! His glamor was gone, and he was fussing in front of the mirror. In fact, he was practicing his stance and his look.

In private, he was just as insecure as me. I was astounded.

I had to unlock the stall and come out. As soon as he saw me, the act started again and the aura reappeared instantly. Washing up, I left the restroom and returned to the front of the bar.

As it crept closer to closing time, Kevin and I got ready to leave. Just as we were thinking about cutting out, here came Tracy and his crew and his mystique was back in full force. I could feel it sliding over everyone around me like a cape of night.

I even slipped under myself again despite my new knowledge. In fact, I found him even sexier now that I knew how hard he worked at it.

As he slipped by my chair, he came by and said, "Call me sometime, Kid." Then a wink and he was gone.

Much Later: Here is an odd bit of synchronicity to follow up this story. One of my friends, who frequently reads these pieces for me, could not do so tonight because he is working a charity function at the LA Eagle. What he does not know is that Tracy was the lead bartender there for many years.

You're The First One Of Those I Ever Met!

This chapter is subtitled "or How Not To Come Out At Work"

My first real job after college was at a mortgage house. Dry as dust and I loved it.

I spent my entire day elbow deep in deed books at the county courthouse researching who did what to whom in 1847 for a little piece of land that should be holding Bob's sheep but was stolen by Tom who wanted to put a chicken coop there. And so it would lie until someone else decided that chicken poop made a great setting for million-dollar condos.

As I said, I loved it.

We all pretty much stuck to ourselves and it was a small office of maybe 20 people. I came in as a temp and stayed.

So, I had been there about six months and it came time for the annual company Christmas party.

Bobbi Jo, the company secretary, called me over to her desk and asked me how many people she should put me down for at the party. Carl and I had only been dating for a month and he would not have been comfortable going to such things with me, so I told her one.

"One?" she drawled. "Surely, a nice boy like you has a girl you could bring."

"Sorry." I shrugged.

"Is there something wrong with you?" poked Bobbi Jo.

"Just haven't found the right girl, yet." I smiled as I tried to get away.

"Well, why don't you ask Carol back in processing?" Bobbi Jo suggested as her mind started to whirl.

I had to get off that matchmaking carousel but fast! I had seen her practically force strangers on awkward dates and did not want to have any part of it.

"That's not necessary..." I started.

"Well, why not? It's not like you have bugs."

Deep breath.

"Bobbi Jo, I won't be taking a woman to the party because I don't date women." I said slowly.

"Well, why not?" she demanded.

"Because I am gay." I said quietly.

"What? You are?"

"Yes, but let's keep it quiet, shall we?" I looked around making sure no one else heard.

"Well, you're the first one of those I ever met!"

This coming from a woman whose hair was standing on her head in a slow-motion tornado. Blue highlights accented it and small feathers were beaded down the ends.

"Ohhhhhhhhhh...I somehow doubt that..." was all I could say.

I should have known better than to think that bubble head could keep a secret. Within a week, everyone knew in the office.

My supervisor called me into his office.

"Mike, I have question for you." he said nervously.

"Yeah, Dan?" No clue in my mind.

"Well, Bobbi Jo has been doing some talking and I wanted to make certain that you felt welcome here."

"What has she been talking about?" I asked as a light bulb went.

"Well, I know the guys over at the courthouse can be kinda rough in their talk and wanted to make sure that you didn't feel that they were talking about you."

"You mean when they call each other "fag"?" I laughed. "Seriously, Dan, thank you for asking but I am perfectly comfortable and prefer the guys to just go on being guys."

"I just want to be sure..."

"I am fine. Really fine."

Things were a bit odd at the deed books for about a week after that but once everyone realized that I wasn't sprouting fangs or spraying glitter, things got back to normal.

Except, Bobbi Jo, that is.

The stereotype for gay men at the time said that all we cared about was hair, makeup and clothes. And Bobbi Jo bought it hook, line and sinker. Every time, I came into the office, I was treated to her latest self-remake in a whirl of hair, nails, clothes and makeup.

The blond tornado was followed by a blue 'do with pink nails. This was replaced by a black shag reminiscent of a cocker spaniel and yellow talons and so it went for months.

Those who know me well would be kind in calling me cosmetically challenged to say the least and I admit to being out of my league, so I would just smile and nod and get away as quickly as I could.

Bangled earrings the size of eggs competed with mirrored nails to catch the eye only to be replaced with crystals that appeared to be from an old chandelier and a dress that would have been at home at the circus.

I think her most astounding outfit had to be the pink chintz sleeveless dress with the plastic hoops inside to keep it rigid and large neon green half balls attached to the skirt. The clear plastic heels only succeeded in making her taller and therefore easier to spot. Bobbi Jo really enjoyed the '80's.

I was her very own caged fairy at her beck and call and she was in heaven.

It ended swiftly.

One morning in late Spring, I followed her up in the elevator. She was being followed by a tall, attractive man carrying several boxes for her. He dropped them by her desk and then kissed her and left. I assumed it was her husband.

Bobbi Jo grabbed me as I was walking in and spread her claws for me to examine.

"See what I did over the weekend?" They were blue and orange tiger striped - how could I miss them? "Roger and me were down at the lake and I got this idea from the latest Banarama video on MTV?"

"Was that Roger who just left?" I asked.

"Yes, that was him." she said.

"You are a very lucky woman." I noted.

"Why's that?" she asked.

"Your husband is a handsome man and you are very lucky."

The switch was instantaneous.

"Now see here. You listen to me. He is my husband." Bobbi Jo started spitting out the words.

"Yeah, I know that."

"You keep your hands and dirty mind off my man." she snapped.

"Of course. I only meant..."

"I know what you meant, you little pansy. HE IS MINE!"

Grabbing my paperwork, I made for the courthouse.

I hoped that she would calm down and it would all go away but that was not Bobbi Jo's style. Come afternoon, my boss, Dan, called me into his office.

"Mike, I have had a complaint filed against you."

"Is this that condo down by the river? I know it is going slowly but we found a whole new train of doc--"

"No, that's not it."

"Then?" I was confused.

"It's Bobbi Jo."

Light bulbs went on.

"What is she saying?"

"Well, you know I have tried to be good about this "gay" thing."

"Sure." I nodded.

"She says you tried to hit on her husband." He started to blush.

"I honestly have never spoken to the man."

"Well she says you did and that she is going to quit unless we fire you." He looked embarrassed. "Now, you do great work, much better than hers actually, so I want to know exactly what happened."

As I told him, he nodded and listened. When I was done, he sat and thought for a moment.

"I pretty much had it figured out. I need you to do me a favor. Gather up your stuff here and meet me at the office at 3. Okay?"

Shit. I was getting fired.

Well, 3 o'clock came around and I showed up with all my gear ready to be terminated. Dan met me in the lobby and asked me to come with him. He led me to his office and had me sit down.

"I will be back in a minute."

My heart beat heavily and I was resigned to being let go.

That is when I heard a commotion in the hallway.

"This is not the last you will hear from me!" I think it was Bobbi Jo!

Slamming drawers and raised voices and then silence for about fifteen minutes.

Dan came back in the office

"Any chance you can take over the processing desk for a few weeks?"

"What about --"

"Let's just say Bobbi Jo chose to leave the company. Very quickly." he said.

"You mean you're not firing me?"

"Why would I fire you? You're not the one who lied to me. Are you up for it?" he asked.

"Sure!'

I even got a raise.

POSTSCRIPT:

Larry and I were sitting in the Garage about six months later sharing a drink when he nudged me.

"Did you see the one who just walked in?" he asked.

Turning, I choked.

It was Roger, Bobbi Jo's husband.

I'm Ready For My Close Up, Mr. Demille!

Does anyone else have an exact date that they can pinpoint when the world took a complete left hard turn and ended up somewhere you never dreamed it would?

Some say when they got married.

Others say when they graduated college.

I have even heard some people say that it was the day that Kennedy was shot.

Mine is July 25, 1985.

It seems like ancient history now.

I think it was a Tuesday.

No bells going off yet?

Let me explain.

I was off early and was meeting Larry at the Garage. I walked in and I could barely recognize the place.

The first oddity was that all the lights were on full. Glaring. You could actually see each other.

All of the bars specialized in discrete half lighting so that the illusion of a hidden wonderland was always there. To have the works lights on meant a shared illusion was in danger and that no one cared.

Add to this the fact that no music was playing, and no one was talking. It was like walking into a wake.

In a manner of speaking, it was.

None of the TV's or video monitors were playing music videos or their normal highly edited porn tapes. Instead, each and every single one of them was turned to the news.

"Rock Hudson announces he is gay and has AIDS." flashed on every screen.

"What?" I started but was shushed immediately.

'MacMillan and Wife' was gay? I had spent hours watching that show as a teenager growing up. Seriously. I could even recite the show's tag lines. Did that warp me somehow?

On the TV screens, helicopters circled a house in the hills above Hollywood as reporters and photographers tried for a glimpse of the "tragic hero".

"Hero, my ass." said the man beside me. "Maybe if he had come out years ago, things might be better for all of us."

By that time, we all knew the statistics, 5,538 already dead of AIDS and an unknown number infected. Anger had been rising but no one would pay attention to a group so hidden in the shadows that cities were even afraid to put the gay pride rallies on the official parade calendars for fear the churches would object.

A test had just been announced about a month before but with a disease that didn't have a cure, did you really want to know? It was a real case of "Damned if you do, damned if you don't".

Even the goddamn president didn't say the word "AIDS" for five years into the epidemic.

So, what are the new channels concentrating on?

"Hudson's stylish mansion is built in the Gothic Revival style…"

"Hudson is well known for the lavish parties he throws…"

Or "Hudson's Yorkies must be wondering at all of the attention…"

Everyone was avoiding the real issue. Why didn't he come out earlier?

But we all knew that answer. Being gay in Hollywood, as elsewhere, could be the kiss of death for a career. Even the guy who invented the machine that defeated the Nazis was hounded to suicide because he was gay.

NEWSFLASH! "Linda Evans spotted slipping into exclusive clinic for AIDS test!"

No one is focusing on the thousands with the disease. The newshounds are focused on an actress who KISSED Hudson in his last TV show.

KISSED?!?

Really?!?

She kissed him, CBS News. She didn't suck his cock!!!

Get some goddamn perspective!

I must admit that I was as engrossed as everyone else.

Larry, with a tired laugh, said "Can you imagine if he had kissed Nancy Reagan?"

(What no one knew then and what did not come out until many years later was that Nancy Reagan knew about Hudson's diagnosis and that she had called the French prime minister when Hudson was in Paris to try to make sure he got the best treatment possible.)

BREAKING NEWS

"Lawsuit Filed Against Hudson by Former Male Lover for Exposing Him to AIDS"

This looked juicy and we all leaned forward.

Anyone should have seen that coming. Lawsuits were a dime a dozen, and everyone was out for their share of the spoils.

BREAKING NEWS

"Fans Claim Hudson not Gay and Caught AIDS from Blood Transfusions"

Did they not read the man's own press release?

"Delusional" was how Larry put it.

And so, it went all night.

Each new flash brought eyes back to the screen as the headlines got seedier and stupider.

I finally started to look around at the bar around me. I had never noticed how dingy the place actually was with all of the lights dim before. Cobwebs and peeling paint competed with stained carpet and ceiling tiles. I even think I saw a cockroach over towards the restrooms.

All I could think of at that time is that Hudson's announcement had turned a huge spotlight to shine on the gay community.

The country was starting to look.

WERE WE READY FOR IT?

Yin Meets Yang

Carl introduced me to Robert and Al late one August afternoon. They lived in a Cape Cod house with an honest to god white picket fence.

Al was the editor and publisher of a local gay newspaper called "Gay Times!" and they need an additional staffer to help cover current events and the arts. Tall and willowy and reminding me vaguely of a ferret, he was also soft spoken and confident as only one who had been through Hell could be.

Al also liked to quote Nietzsche. "That which does not kill us makes us stronger." was a favorite phrase of his.

Al's family had found out he was gay at 17 and had thrown him out. He survived by living on the couches of friends and graduated high school while homeless. That didn't kill him.

He persisted.

Al worked 60 hours a week while he applied to colleges. He dragged himself back to a friend's couch just long enough to catch an hour's sleep before his next job. That didn't kill him.

He got accepted.

Al borrowed used textbooks from the library and friends when he could not afford them. He often would sleep in the library hoping not to get caught. That did not kill him.

He graduated at the top of his class.

Al was not someone you crossed lightly, and he was a friend you wanted to have. He reigned over everyone like Papa Smurf protecting his flock. I liked him immediately.

Robert, on the other hand, was shy and reserved. Thin, wispy and a pencil mustache, he couldn't have weighed more than 150. It was difficult to get him to talk but when you did, and he smiled, the room lit up.

Al was always in command of any situation and had a crowd around him bustling and hustling. I have never known a man to have that many projects going at once and have all of them come in on time. He was a model of efficiency.

Robert, on the other hand, was the ultimate worker bee. Simply wind him up and let him go. Need a house painted? Al bought the paint and Robert had it done - that day. Zip! Zip! Zip!

They fit together like two pieces of a puzzle and could never imagine life apart.

But Robert had his hidden side as well. He would suddenly disappear, and no one could find him. A whiff of incense always hung around him when he reappeared. He would come back all sweaty. And his eyes would be shiny. Finally, I followed him upstairs when he wasn't looking. He slipped into the attic and was gone.

I listened at the door to the attic and heard odd noises. Rhythmic noises ending with an outtake of breath and a quick moan. And something sounded like chains rattling.

Intrigued, I opened the door and slipped up.

Colors assaulted the eyes as movies posters and Chinese lanterns lit the upper chamber. Num-chuks and throwing stars lined the walls and a huge punching bag swung back and forth as Robert kicked and punched it.

"Whoa!" came out involuntarily. Robert turned and smiled.

"Like it? Welcome to the Bruce Lee Room!"

"What is all this stuff?" I asked looking around.

Robert lit up as he explained to me that he owned the world's largest collection of Bruce Lee Memorabilia. He even had certifications showing that he held the record. Movie posters competed with signed photos which vied with movie props that crowded out costumes covering every inch of the walls.

The gem of his collection was the actual cat suit worn by Bruce Lee in his movie "Game of Death" The best part about it was that it actually fit Robert. He tried it on and let me feel it.

"How did you get this?" I asked. It was a vaguely Muppet-like bright yellow cloth and looked like something better suited to a surfer than an action flick.

"I found it at a show and outbid everyone else."

"Wow!"

"Yeah, I wore it for a week everywhere." he said.

"You did? Didn't anyone say anything?" I asked.

"Of course, they did. Some big guy even tried to take it from me." Robert answered.

"How big was he?"

"About six foot, five."

"What happened?"

"I beat the shit out of him."

Did I mention that Robert was a fourth level black belt?

Sex With Nuns

"Micheal, stop giggling!" came the whisper over my shoulder.

"I can't help it, Larry! A nun with a dildo is just funny."

"Have some decorum. This is not the Eagle on a Saturday night." he answered.

"But that is a real nun. And, that is a real dildo."

And, she was. And, it was.

My first assignment for "Gay Times!" had been for a fried and I to attend the first safe sex seminar to be given by the local AIDS task force. Several hundred gay men were invited, and it was being held in a hotel ballroom. It sounded kind of fun and even a bit titillating.

Until we found out who had volunteered to run it and that we were in the front row.

Father Tim was a local priest whom we all knew walked the pink side of the altar so to speak but we never talked about it. Tall and imposing, he had a hefty baritone and belly laugh sure to wake the saints.

Him, we could handle. It was the three nuns with him that were the, um, problem.

Sister Andrea was, well, the best term to use is, a stereotypical lesbian. She was in control and she knew it. All she needed was a flannel shirt to be out tooling with the Dykes on Bikes.

Sister Catherine (or "Cate" as she preferred to be called) was more matronly. She reminded everyone in the room of their grandmother. The grandmother you never EVER wanted to disappoint.

And finally, Sister Elizabeth was a young and shy young woman. She was also very clearly ill at ease discussing anything having to do with sex. She actually blushed whenever she said the word.

In short, the four of them were a case of the blind leading the blinded so to speak. Or would a virgin leading the whores be a better analogy?

It started off easily enough with a discussion about various venereal diseases. Slides showed pictures of dripping and oozing body parts that should never have existed in nature. Some of them I had never even heard of and hoped to never hear of again. (What is "elephantiasis" again?)

Through if all, Father Tim tried to get us all to respond. The nuns clearly expected us to listen in rapt attention and we really did our best.

Then, began the actual "safe sex" part of the lecture.

Sister Andrea made a point of telling us how we had to be so careful with our penises because they really are the root of all evil.

("As if she had ever seen one in real life." I muttered to a quick "shush" from beside me.)

"Always make certain to grasp the penis firmly around the base."

(A number of choking sounds came from across the rooms that turned into quick coughing fits as elbows lashed out.)

"Make certain that you don't allow it to leak as this may decrease the sexual excitement."

("Not always!" came softly from my right.)

That is when the dildos made their appearance. "Cate" made a point of handling them out to every two of us to practice with.

("I've seen bigger!" was repeated throughout the room. "We all have!" was the response under our breaths.)

"Unroll the condom carefully and slide it over the head of the penis." she instructed in the same tone of voice Julia Child would have used when describing how to truss a chicken.

That is when we discovered that the dildos were Magnum sized and the condoms were not.

Clearing her throat, Sister Cate said "Of course, they will fit. Just push a little harder."

(I was trying to keep from bursting out laughing so hard that I was about to pass out from lack of air. My friend just kept pushing that dildo into the condom as hard as he could.)

"Don't worry about pushing too hard as they usually stretch." said Sister Cate as she demonstrated by manhandling a monster dildo so hard that it ripped through the condom and went sailing across the stage.

That was Sister Elizabeth's cue to start talking about personal lubricants. She was so softly spoken then everyone had to lean in to try to catch her words.

"Water-based lubricants are always the best but they sometimes dry out and fail to work."

("Just like a man!" mumbled behind my back.)

"Silicon based lubes are good because they never stop working." she continued. "They have to be wiped off."

("The best things always do." got shushed to my left.)

"If you have trouble, use more lubricant." she whispered.

("Does she realize that some of these boys could drive a Mack truck through a keyhole?" triggered giggles behind me.)

"Now let's talk about fetishes." boomed Father Tim...and so it went for the entire afternoon.

Foot fetishes led to food play to leather to S&M. Or "the Sado-Masochism" as he put it.

By the end of the afternoon, we were all rung out from laughing.

We also gave them a standing ovation.

I Don't Think You Are Taking This Seriously!

It's amazing how the more things change, the more they stay the same. Recently, a good friend had something happen that was so similar to an incident earlier in my life that I just had to write about when this happened to me.

Did I ever tell you about the time that I was charged with sexual harassment?

Due to a slowdown in the economy, the title agency had laid me off and I had taken a job as that most hated of all creatures - a bill collector. I spent my days calling people who could not pay their bills so that I could pay my own. It was not exactly what I would call glamorous, but it did, yes, pay my bills.

Our office was this enormous room with several thousand people in it seated at identical desks with identical phones wearing identical headsets reading identical scripts ...SNORE...Ooops! You get the idea.

After my misadventures with Bobbie Jo at the title agency, I had decided to be a little more discrete about my private life. In such a large anonymous company, there really was no reason for my being gay to come up. It was Ohio, after all.

My supervisor was Loretta. The moment I met her my Gaydar went completely wild. It wasn't just that she was wearing blue jeans and hiking boots. Add to that blouses that were as close to flannel lumberjack shirts as you could get at Ann Taylor and hair cut in a perfectly ladylike Marine crew-cut and I definitely had her number.

And, as soon as she looked me up and down, she also had mine. My magician friend, Henry Best, has nothing on Gaydar when it comes to mind reading.

Anyway, after a few months, my numbers were really good. So good in fact that they were talking to me about management. One of the steps to management was reviewing calls of team members for accuracy, proper policy, disclaimers and the lot.

I was given a list of random calls and I would listen to them and then compare them to a checklist. Pretty basic. Did they make it or not?

Then, I had to review several calls from Mandy.

Mandy was a divorced mother of two who sat several desks down from me. I knew her well enough to ask how her kids were each morning as I walked by and that was about it.

She was certainly not what I would call beautiful. Tall, thin and with one breast noticeably larger than the other and a bottom the size of Manhattan added up to a picture of someone who could not be called classically attractive. And her whiny voice buzzed adenoidally like a mosquito.

Anyway, I had reviewed several hundred calls by the time I got to hers. Honestly, she sucked. Really sucked. She sounded not only bored but boring and was anything but a "people" person.

However, none of this was for me to decide. All I did was fairly review her calls according to the checklist and turn my reports weekly over to Loretta. Then, never gave it a thought.

Until -

Loretta met with each of us monthly to review our progress and to tell us how we could improve. Mine always went well so I never thought twice about them.

Mandy's did not. In fact, she was put on notice to improve or she would be let go. She was mad, and she wanted revenge.

She couldn't take it out on Loretta, so she needed another target.

The first that I knew something was going on was when both Loretta and I were summoned to the Human Resources Department. Loretta was clearly as puzzled as I and kept saying: "What have you done?"

The HR Lady, Karen was a rather sallow faced woman wearing glasses that only succeeded in making her look even more like Woodsy Owl. She ushered us in with the air of someone with far better things to be doing.

"I am sorry to have to bring you in here, but I have had a very serious complaint about you." she said primly.

"Me? What did I do? Did a client complain?"

"No, this is more serious. As you know, we here at Advance Collections take sexual harassment very seriously." continued Karen in a very serious voice.

"Yes?" What did this have to do with me?

"One of your coworkers has accused you of making unwanted advances." continued Karen.

"What?!?" Did one of the guys think I was hitting on them?

"Yes, she said that you have been harassing her to meet her after work -"

"She? SHE!?!" I interrupted.

Clearly irritated by my interruption, Karen went on. "Yes, she stated that on several occasions, you came by her desk and -"

This is when Loretta started to loudly snort.

"- tried to ask her over to your home." a tight-lipped Karen tried to get out.

That did it. Loretta just started ripping out with huge guffaws.

"May I ask what is so funny?" snapped Karen.

Choking, Loretta tried to get it out. "You think -" SNORT "he tried to -" CHORTLE "ask a WOMAN out?" She then dissolved in laughter.

Confused, Karen could only stare.

"I believe that I can handle this in two words." I began.

"Go ahead!" threw Karen at me.

"I'm gay."

"What?" queried the uncomprehending HR lady.

"I am gay."

"That's actually three words." interjected Loretta before dissolving once more into laughs.

"I don't think you are taking this seriously." iced out Karen.

"I am taking this very seriously. I am gay." I forced out.

"Listen -" she started.

"No, listen to me. I am gay! I sleep with men! I am queer! I DO NOT DATE WOMEN!"

Loretta could not stop laughing. I was afraid that she would pass out.

"But, Mandy said -" started Karen before realizing she had let something slip.

"Mandy? I should have known." I stood. "Now listen very carefully! I AM A BIG FLAMING FAG!"

Her bubble burst, the HR rep could just sit there.

"Now, is there anything else?"

Silence.

"If that is all, I have work to do. Good day!"

I never saw Mandy again after that day.

What the Hell Is Gaydar?

"Gaydar is a myth!" insisted Mark.

The three of us were sitting outside Kat zinger's Deli watching the Saturday afternoon crowd going by.

"It is absolutely real." said Larry.

"Prove it!" said Mark.

You could almost hear "Dance of the Hours" start up as Larry began doing his best Madeleine Kahn impression at the stream of passersby.

"Yes…no.no.no.no.no.no…Yes…no.no…Yes…no.no…Yes…no.no.no.no. no.no.no.no.no.no."

"What?"

"Shh…Yes!...no.no.no.no.no…Yes…no.no.no.no.no.no.no…Yes..no.no…Yes…no.no.no.no.no.no.no.no.no.no.no.no…Wait!...YES!!!!"

Sounding disgusted, Mark said "That proves nothing. This is German Village after all. I would be surprised if half of these men WEREN'T gay."

"What is Gaydar?" I asked.

Both of them looked at me as though I was insane.

"You really don't know?" asked Larry.

"No, not really."

"Micheal, sometimes I forget how sheltered you really are. Gaydar is the inherent ability of a gay man to tell if someone else is gay or not." said Larry.

"How does it work?"

"Have you ever just known someone was looking at you."

"Yes."

"Gaydar!"

"Or damn good peripheral vision." Chimed in Mark.

"Hush!" said Larry. "Have you ever known someone was gay before you even met them?"

"Sort of…"

"Gaydar!"

Mark loudly stage coughed "Bullshit!"

"Okay, unbeliever. How would you like me to prove to you that gaydar exists?" asked Larry.

"Okay, the next person that come through the door that you think is gay, I want you to get his phone number." challenged Mark.

"Fine."

About a dozen people walked by until Larry said. "Him!" and gestured towards a man in jeans and a t shirt.

'That is too easy. His T Shirt says "Born to Burn Hair!" said Mark.

"Okay, let's try again!"

Four more people walked by until he grunted "That one!" towards a stout man in a ball cap.

"Cheater!" said Mark.

"Why?" asked Larry.

"Like I can't see the earring and that the hat says "DC Eagle"?" pointed out Mark.

"All right…" Larry said again scanning the crowd.

Finally, a father walked by with four kids in tow.

"That one. Definitely."

"The breeder?" exclaimed Mark. "Now I know you are shitting me."

"Him."

"He has kids."

"And…?"

"He has kids!"

"I could have kids. You never know."

"Like you ever slept with a woman." quipped Larry.

Mark snorted. "Anyway, there is no way to prove your theory." as he nodded towards the man in line.

"I would not be so sure if I were you." said Larry and he slipped off to join the people in line waiting for the counter man to order.

Fascinated, I watched Larry work. He was in line directly after the man with the four young children. For a moment, nothing happened and then Larry "accidentally" brushed into the man.

Apologizing, Larry struck up a conversation. Chatting with the man, he offered to hold the youngest child while the man paid for his order. After the man departed, Larry came back to the table with a fresh coffee.

"And?" asked Mark.

"His name is Paul and here is his business card."

"Was he gay?" purred Mark.

"Turns out he and his wife just split. They were both sleeping with the same man and she ran off with the other guy leaving him with the kids."

"I don't believe that as far as I can throw you."

"Believe it or not, I have a date tomorrow night."

"Cool!" I interjected.

"Cool, nothing." said Mark. "How do I know you didn't know him before?"

"Foul unbeliever!" answered Larry, pointing at Mark. "How am I going to prove it to you?"

"Well, I don't believe you as far as I can throw you so let's put your Mike to work here."

"Me?" I squeaked.

"Yes, you. If this Gaydar is so powerful, and if every gay guy has it, then surely you must, too." went on Mark.

"That's not fair. He's barely out of the closet." sighed Larry.

"Either we test it using him or you admit it does not exist."

"I don't know…" I started.

"Hush, Micheal. It will all be fine. So, what is the test?"

"We have the boy here scan the crowd and if he tells us someone is gay, you have to get their number."

"Interesting…"

"Chickening out?" purred Mark.

"Hell, no." shot back Larry. "Challenge accepted."

"Wha?"

"Just start looking, Micheal. Watch everybody as they come in and tell me if you think they are gay."

Five minutes passed.

"This is silly."

"Keep going."

About a dozen people passed. I felt some twinges but nothing I would stake a bet on. Finally, a pair of bicycle cops parked their bikes and walked in. One was taller and blond. The other was shorter and dark haired and –

That internal alarm went OFF! WOOT! WOOT! WOOT! A-OOO-GAH! DIVE! DIVE! DIVE!

"I know that look." said Larry. "Who?"

"The short cop."

"Really? I would have thought the taller one."

"Does it matter? The boy said the short cop?" pushed Mark.

"Then the short cop it is!" continued Larry as he wandered off.

Again, he pulled the same trick. Standing in line behind the two cops, he accidentally bumped the shorter one. He then apologized and continued talking to the officer. Laughing, he pointed to us and continued talking. Finally, he came back to the table.

"And?" asked Mark.

"And, what?" innocently answered Larry.

"You know damn well what. Did you get the cop's number? Was little Mike here right?"

"Oh, yeah. I did." he smiled while waving about the piece of paper.

That's amazing!" I said.

Loudly clearing his throat, Mark walked off.

"Do you want to hear really amazing?" asked Larry.

"Sure."

"He asked me to give you his number."

Mr. Hobbs, Have You Been Drinking?

I saw the flashing lights in the rear-view mirror start up.

Shitshitshitshitshitshitshshitshitshitshitshitshit!

I slid the bottle of vodka under the passenger seat and pulled over.

SHIT!

I drive drunk for the only time in my life and now I am going to jail!!!

WHY DID I PUT THAT GODDAMN RAINBOW STICKER ON THE CAR?????

****

It was a Monday morning when the call came through.

"Micheal?"

"Dad?"

"Yeah."

My anxiety level shot through the roof.

"What's wrong?"

"We were trying to call you at home last night."

"I got home kind of late from the lake."

"It's your Grandmother, Son." His voice sounded odd.

"What's wrong?" I asked as my heart dropped.

"Your grandmother passed away night before last, Son." Pause. "She had a heart attack."

My own heart skipped a beat.

"Who found her?"

"Your Uncle Richard said she wasn't feeling well and didn't go to church. When he came back from some errands, he couldn't wake her."

"Are you okay, Dad?" I asked as I eased onto a bench.

"I'll be fine. It just is a bit of a shock."

"What do you need me to do?"

"Well, Micheal, the viewing is tonight. I need you to be there."

"Of course. What time and where?"

"6:00 at Schoedinger's."

"Okay. I'll be there."

After hanging up, I tried to pull myself together. And failed miserably. Somehow the rest of the day passed. Then I did the thing that any good grandson does when under stress.

I got drunk. VEEEEEEEEEEERY drunk!

I headed to my favorite bar and ordered shots of ouzo. And told the bartender why I was drinking. He bought me a couple rounds himself. But I got toasted!!!

Then, I compounded that with an even worse faux pas.

I drove.

Oh, yeah.

Somehow, I swung by the apartment and grabbed my suit but just could not get my tie to knot for some reason. I mean I tried but the knot never looked quite right, and it refused to loop evenly. But, it would just have to do.

Anyway, so I am driving to the funeral home with the radio playing full blast and drunk off my mind. Schoedinger's was the Hobbs funeral home of choice and I could have driven there blindfolded.

Which was a very good thing as I was blind drunk.

****

Slowly the officer got out of his car and slid up to the car.

I watched him in the rearview mirror as he approached. He was smoking hot! Buzz cut, tight uniform, little mustache, and mirrored glasses. Did he just walk out of the Village People?

Then, I felt a pang of guilt. "Oh, My God! I am on my way to a funeral and I am cruising a cop!"

"License and registration, please!"

I handed the documents to him and waited.

"Mr. Hobbs, do you know why I stopped you?"

"No, sirrrr."

"One of your tail lights is out and needs replaced...."

That must have been about the time he caught a whiff of my breath.

"Mr. Hobbs, have you been drinking?"

That is when I broke down crying.

"Yes, siiiiiiiiiiir. (BAWLING!) My Grandma died. (SOB!) And they have her at Schoedinger's (snot running) and I have to go see her."(WAAAAAH!)

This is when I completely lost it.

The cop looked at me for a minute then leaned in and put his hand on my shoulder.

"Mr. Hobbs, this is what we are going to do. We are only about six blocks from the funeral home. You are going to drive there. I am going to follow you. Once we get there, I want you to park the car and go inside. Once inside, you will give someone else your keys and not drive anymore tonight. Is that clear?"

"Yes, siiiiiiiir." (SNIFFLES!)

He handed me my keys back and then followed me as I started the car moving again. He even followed me into the funeral home's parking lot. Then, as I got out of the car he pulled up beside me.

"I'm sorry for your loss. Here." He handed me a piece of paper and drove off.

I looked at the paper. It was his phone number. Could this day get any weirder?

So anyway, I stumbled into the funeral parlor. Finding the right room, I opened the doors and walked in. Near the front of the room was a closed casket and two figures standing nearby. It was Uncle Dan and Dad.

"Dad?"

My Dad came up to me with a very strange look on his face.

"Son, have you been drinking?"

"Just a little, Dad."

"Oh, Son."

With a sigh, he pulled me into the men's room.

"Son, clean yourself up and come back." He said returning to the chapel.

Oh, My God! No wonder he knew I was drunk, I thought as I looked in the mirror. Not only was my hair messed up, but I also had only gelled half my hair so one side was straight and the other side spiked. In addition, my tie was uneven and looped only under one side of my collar. My shirt hung out on one side and I had missed a few buttons.

"I'm such an idiot!" I thought. Retying my tie and somehow getting my hair under control, I forced myself to stand up straight and tried to sober up.

I splashed water in my face and stared at my own face.

"Now, you are going to go out there and make sure no one figures out you are drunk." I told myself.

I stumbled into a chair and handed the keys to the car to Carol, a distant cousin. Carol was a butch one, she was. She was built like a tank and there was no fooling her.

"Micheal, have you been drinking?", she growled.

"Sort of." I said. "You mind driving?"

As the funeral progressed. Carol put her arm around me and I bawled.

"You know your Grandma knew all about you." she said.

"What are you talking about?"

"You know, gay!" she went on.

"Me?" I had told very few people at that time.

"I heard her ask your father."

"But she never said anything to me."

"What could she say? She didn't approve but what could she say."

MY GRANDMA KNEW?

"Mamie was a good Methodist woman but you were her blood. She loved you."

I swear it wasn't the alcohol as I started to cry. I felt a furry, mannish arm squeeze me.

"Micheal," said Carol, "besides times are changing. "

We spent the rest of the evening dishing on the family and talking about all of the family secrets. Carol was a good old girl.

The next day, my hangover clouded the entire service. Thank god Carol drove to the cemetery.

But, the week after Grandma died, I marched in the Gay Pride Parade. Thousands of people lined the street. It was amazing.

And me?

I carried a huge sign and marched.

The sign?

It read, "MY GRANDMA KNEW I WAS GAY AND SHE LOVED ME ANYWAY!"

I miss her still.

Are You Speaking English?
Subtitled: The Gay Dictionary

One of the most important things that I had to learn when I first came out is that gay men in the 80's spoke in short hand all their own.

Seriously, there were times when I knew I was hearing the words in English, but I wanted to know if they were using telepathy. Eventually, I learned.

Phrase	Meaning
30 Day Virgin	Has not had sex in a while
4:20 Friendly	Marijuana friendly
AC/DC	Bisexual
Angel	Airline pilot who is cruising the bar
Auntie Mame	Effeminate wealthy older gay man
A-Word	AIDS
Basket Shopping	Looking at men's crotches
Bathed at the Club	Had anonymous sex
Butt Pirate	Gay man
Chapstick Lesbian	Athletic Lesbian
Cherry	Virgin
Chicken	Underage kid looking for sex
Chicken Hawk	Older man looking for younger
Cleaning The Kitchen	Douching
Disco Duck	Someone who THINKS they can

	dance.
Doggie	Sex on all fours
Doing the Mambo	Had sex
Fag Hag	Women who hang around with gay men
Fairy Godfather	Watches over younger men
Fullback	Automatically flips to the bottom
Gaelic	Oral sex
Girl Scout	Military man off duty and cruising
Going to Pittsburgh	He likes stinky armpits.
Golden Showers	Someone who likes being peed on
Grizzly Adams	Furry guy
Had Dessert	Had sex
Had Tea	Had sex
Has Fleas	A truly ugly man
Has Visitors	Crabs
Joan	A man who is overly groomed
Job Interview	Had sex
Learning French	Making Out
Liberace	Bitchy queen
Lipstick Lesbian	Model by day, Harley by night.
Lounge Lizard	Same bar every night
Met John Doe	Had sex but can't remember their

	name
Morning Walk	Waking up at a sex partner's home
Morning Wood	Erect in the morning
Muscle Queen	Butch in the gym but has a purse fall out of their mouth.
Oh, My…	That was stupid.
Oh, My!	You're a moron.
OH, MY!!!	You're a fucking moron!
One Eyed Trouser Snake	A Penis
Pencil Sharpener	Performer of oral sex
Peppery	My God! He needs a shower!
Peroxide Poisoning	We know that is not your normal color.
Pink Triangle Boy	Gay man
Playing Horse	Had sex
Playing the Banjo	Masturbation
Plays with Barbie	Drag queen lover
Poppers	Inhalants
Quarterback	Top in gay sex
Queen Victoria	A Royal Bitch
Rides Both Sides	Bisexual
Speaking French	Having Sex
Spoke On The Phone	Had Sex

Sugar Daddy	Older man supporting a younger one
Temporary Roommate	Venereal Disease
Tipping Bird	Performer of oral sex
Tossing Salad	Oral-Anal sex
Went On A Date	Had Sex

You Broke WHAT?

Larry sighed and handed me the ice pack.

"Now, tell me. How did you get a black eye?" he asked

"Do I really have to?" I placed the pack on my eye.

"From the top…"

"Okay." I sighed.

I had been asked to deliver copies of "Gay Times" to several local businesses close to my old apartment on First Avenue. You know, a couple of bars, a restaurant and…an adult bookstore.

The Adult-ADULT-ADULT!!! Bookstore used to be north of Ohio State campus on High Street and was just down from a couple of shady bars and a "burlesque" show bar. Bright neon signs proclaimed "ADULT NOVELTIES" and "VIDEO BOOTHS" as well as a glass door covered with bars.

To say the least, it was not a welcoming environment. Especially for someone like me. In other words, someone who had never gone into an adult bookstore before.

I was an adult bookstore virgin at the age of 22. I had never even seen a porn film. So gulping and gripping my newsletters, I walked in. And immediately entered a maze painted black and lit by neon lights from overhead. Ominously, the door clicked behind me.

There must have been quite some treasures being guarded as it took forever to find my way through the labyrinth. I expected to encounter the Minotaur at any moment.

Finally, I came to another metal door and went through into the store and

---

Was totally disappointed.

I wasn't quite sure what I expected but an overly bright room vaguely reminiscent of a KMART kitchen display was not it. Fluorescent lights screamed from above and shelves chock full of the sum of human perversion in neat rows was nowhere near what I had envisioned.

"Just warning you, now. I got a baseball bat under the counter." came from behind the counter.

I am not sure which was scarier: the clerk's giant pink Mohawk or the incredible number of piercings in his face. He actually clanked as he spoke. He was so short I could barely see his eyes over the counter.

"I have your papers."

"Oh, put them over there." he said vaguely pointing.

"I'm curious. Why the maze?" I asked as I added the papers to an overflowing table.

"We've been robbed so many times that it confuses them. That gives me a chance to hit the button under the counter that locks the doors on both ends. Makes it easier for the cops." he shrugged again.

"You've really been robbed?"

"Twice this month." the clerk answered wistfully as if he missed the excitement.

My mission accomplished I decided to look around as my curiosity was just plain killing me.

The display directly in front of me was labeled TOYS. It seemed to be a collection of dildos. They ranged from tiny to medium to large to WHOA NELLY! Honestly, there was one that was at least three feet long and a good eight inches around. How could anyone use something like that? What are you going to do? Make a lamp out of it?

The next display was for something called The Wiggler. It looked like a finger protector and was bright purple. And it was battery powered? That is when I triggered it and it started vibrating across the table.

Ah, the box showed the proper usage. The Wriggler went on your tongue but what were you supposed to do…OH! Hmmm. I would be afraid of swallowing it.

Bullwhips? BULLWHIPS! That's just a little too much S in my S and M, thank you very much.

That is when I came to the magazines. Those I had seen before but none quite like these. One was "GOZANGAS!". The cover article talked about the coming 3-D revolution in porn and was titled "Coming at You!"

I could not believe the sheer breadth of the perversion on display. Straight, gay, bisexual, trisexual, omnisexual, vegisexual…you name it.

I accidentally picked up one called "Puppy Love". What? OHMYGOD!!! Dropping it I quickly looked for somewhere to wash my hands.

I am not saying I had not seen gay magazines. I had but the number on display simply blew away the one or two "Blue Boys" I had picked up on the sly. Hmmm.

"Playguy". Hairless wonders.

"Vixens". Drag queens…no.

"Hammer Time". Those are some mighty big hammers all right!

"Buns!" Wow! Those are some yeasty rolls.

The magazine section bled into the video section. I didn't own a VCR but still wanted to see what was offered.

Didn't any of the guys who made porn have hair on their bodies? Seriously, every chest was bare. More than half of them had their entire bodies shaved. A few even had clearly waxed their brows to the point that they resembled Joan Crawford more than Charles Atlas.

Then, I found the COLT section. Masculine, hairy men. Now, we got it going. The huge men on display made me realize exactly how small and puny I was.

A familiar face caught my eye. Traci! He really did work for them as rumor claimed. The movie was entitled "Fur and Leather". Niiiiice.

Without realizing it, I had brushed up against the end of the video aisle. Turning, I saw a sign that said "Video Booths: 25 cents for five minutes." Titillated, I figured why not?

All but one of the booths was occupied so I slipped into it. Locking the door, I sat on the bench and looked around. The booth was tiny and a little smelly. A TV was set into one wall and the room was poorly paneled. There was even a hole in the paneling behind the door.

In for a pound, in for a dollar. I dropped a quarter into the slot and the video began to play. It was a little fuzzy but showed two men doing what men do with each other when alone. It was not well filmed, and the story certainly lacked depth but the impact was unmistakable. I was entranced. I don't know how many quarters I dropped into the machine but time flew by.

Suddenly and without notice, a gigantic male member came through the hole in the wall from the next booth over.

"Aiiighh!" I chirped and flung the door open to run out. The door hit the surprise guest and screams of pain began coming from the next video booth. The door sprung back and tripped me, so I fell face first into a display and cracked my forehead. Picking myself up, and ignoring the moans from the next booth, I ran out through the store.

The pink Mohawked dwarf was just emerging from behind the counter holding his baseball bat as I ran by.

"Wha-?" he started but I was in no place to answer.

Running through the maze and hitting practically every wall, I finally found the door. Rushing out, I was just in time as I heard the door lock behind me.

****

"Oh, my, Micheal. Haven't you ever heard of 'gloryholes'?" sighed Larry.

"I thought they were things you find in seedy rest stops."

"So, you really broke someone's penis?"

"Probably…"

"Micheal, you're an idiot." He grinned. "Don't ever change."

When A Tree Falls In the Forest ...

Gallows humor really can be funny. Seriously, having a man with his arm in a cast tell you he did it by beating off too much actually can make you smile.

Other times, you feel like a complete and utter ass.

One Thanksgiving night, I was at Al and Robert's working on "Gay Times" when I heard IT - the worst joke ever created.

Al's ulcer had been acting up, so he was sitting on the couch pontificating on the evils of spicy food.

"I think that I am handling the curse of bulimia well, don't you?" he asked.

"Bulimia? Isn't that where cheerleaders puke?"

"That's the one. Every pizza, pop, burger or fry taste so good going down. I just wished they tasted the same coming back up."

"Gross!"

"But there is a good point."

"There is?" I asked

"Sure! I haven't fit in these jeans in years." he said while modeling in the mirror.

"I would just hate to be doing it the same way."

Al chuckled.

"If you can't laugh at yourself, who can you laugh at?" he continued.

"Those jokes are so bad. How can people laugh about illness?"

"Sometimes, there is nothing left to do but laugh." he continued. "I mean when I was sitting homeless in a shelter do you know what we laughed about?"

"No."

"The fact that the rich people coming through all smelled like Lysol." Al smiled "And they did."

"Why?"

"I guess they thought that serving us holiday meals was sure to give them leprosy."

"As if."

"Gallows humor, my boy." he grinned. "When all else fails, at least have fun."

"Riiiiiiight."

"Hey! Do you want to hear the world's worst joke?" Al asked.

"Really? The world's worst?" I asked.

"Oh, yes." he smiled like a shark.

"Okay, this I gotta hear."

With a flourish, he stood up.

"Tell me. Have you heard about the Miracle of AIDS?"

"What? Oh, no!"

"Really… Have you heard about the Miracle of AIDS?" he asked.

"No, I haven't."

"It's the only thing that can turn a fruit into a vegetable!" he finished.

"That's awful!"

"Yeah, but it's funny, isn't it?" Al started to giggle.

Despite myself, I found myself starting to giggle and had to suppress it.

"No…"

"Laugh, boy."

And we did. It was gallows humor at its worst. We chortled until we got it all out. Then we sat there in silence for moment.

Finally, Al turned to me and said, "I just want you to know I have it."

"It?"

"AIDS."

And Now We Present...THE PERSONALS

Before the Internet.

Before chat rooms

There were … THE PERSONALS.

I was helping with editing "Gay Times" when Al came up to me and asked me if I could review some of the copy with him.

"Sure. What part?"

"Well, the personals. I got a few complaints and I wanted to check them out." he explained.

"Complaints?" I asked.

"Yes, some of the people said that what we printed was not what they sent us." Al commented.

"Here's the pile of ads. I must be honest. It was a bit difficult to read some of them."

The rules were simple. We took what they sent us and edit it down to 100 characters or less. In the days before email, the letters would come typed or handwritten and then we would do our best to interpret them.

"Okay." Al began. "Here's the first one. What does the add read for this one?"

"Let's see. Oh, that one was a little hard to read. *'Fem, seeks bike for fun, Dutch preferred.'* I read.

"I interpret that one as *'FEMALE, seeks DYKE for fun. BUTCH preferred.'*" said Al.

"Are you sure?"

"Yeah, I think so. What's the next one?" he continued.

"Rich pullet seeks chicken farmer." I read from the edited ad.

"Really? What does the original say?" he asked.

"I had some trouble interpreting that one. It reads, 'Ready for a roll in the hay? Loaded man seeks big farmboy with +++cock to help me plow.'"

"Hmmmm. Try 'Horny bottom seeks man with huge cock.'" Al interpreted.

"Is that what it means?"

"Ye-upp."

I grabbed a stack of the forms.

"Al, the typewritten ones aren't as bad but how about this one? It looks practically like Morse Code."

"Let me see." he asked reaching out.

I handed over the form. It read. "SbBttm, 24, Psc, Sks BBM with JOB, NoDr, 420, GL, Msc, NoC2H5OH."

"That is a hard one." Al puzzled.

"All that I recognize is the word 'Job' and I think he is 24. If it is a he."

"I think so." Al pondered. "Try this 'Submissive Bottom, 24, Pisces, Seeks Big Black Man with Job, No Drama, 4:20 friendly, Good Looking, Muscular, No Drama, Nondrinker.'"

"Is that what that means? I thought it was Windex. Hmm. Okay."

Al and I worked our way through the list until we came to the last one.

"What about this one? My interpretation is 'Ample Candy Lover seeks Interior decorating Beatle lover.'" I asked.

"Really? What does the original say?" asked Al.

"I had to cut it down as the original was too long. It said, 'Plus sized, Chocolate Lover seeks man with experience with glass tables to help me with the Magical Mystery Tour.'"

Al turned pale.

"Umm-hmm. You know I don't think we are going to be printing that one." he said as he tossed the form.

"Oh? We have the room." I asked.

"It has nothing to do with space. I just don't want to print that. Do we have any hand sanitizer?" he began looking around.

"Then why?"

"Let's just say it's not our type of ad." Al said as he stared at me to make sure I got the point.

"You mean- "

"Ye-upp." he drawled.

"That's gross!" I said as we both dashed to the bathroom to wash our hands.

"Ye-upp!"

"Where do we get these people?"

POSTSCRIPT

If you don't get it, Google "coprophilia" and "table".

Livin' La Vida Loco...

My first apartment was in what could best be described as a "dicey" area. In the mid '80's, Parsons Avenue was not exactly the height of safety and sophistication in Columbus.

Appalachians tended to be the main people living in the neighborhood and it was not uncommon for cars cruising by to be playing Lynyrd Skynryd at full blast on the stereo while clouds of marijuana smoke drifted out the windows of the beat-up jalopies they were driving.

My friends called it "The Holler".

I really loved that apartment and was hesitant about moving when Carl suggested it was time for us both to live together.

Then I came out the door one morning and found Marie sitting on my front porch.

You may think me rude but when I find a 250 lbs. woman stuffed into a tube top for someone at least 100 lbs. lighter and certainly ten years younger with dangly earrings and eight-inch stilettos, the word "hooker" does come to mind. Don't ask me why.

Anyway, she was sitting on my front stoop and had her shoes off while she rubbed her feet.

"Pardon me," I said as tried to get around her.

"That's okay, honey. You ain't bothering me." she replied.

"You live around here?"

Tapping her cigarette, she replied, "I'm a little farther out on Livingston but you go where the work is." she said with a wink.

I couldn't help but notice that she had a rather large bag with her that appeared to contain a towel and several other smaller bags.

"Work?" I squeaked.

"Let's just say I am an entertainer." she continued slyly. "I'm Marie."

"Mike."

"Well, Mike, I hope you don't mind my being here."

"No skin off my back." I flipped.

"Yeah, I kinda use this porch as my base for my business. And I promise to be quiet."

Visions of the nightly social life of my porch started to flash through my mind.

"Well, I work nights and haven't heard anything."

"I do try to be a good neighbor." she smiled. "You wanna toke?"

"Toke?"

"Yeah, pot is good, but this stuff is better." Marie said as she held out a small glass container with white powder in the bottom and a butane lighter. My heart skipped a beat.

"They call it Crack but I call it Heaven." she sighed.

A horn sounded.

"Oops, that's my 3 o'clock! Gotta run!" Marie yelled as she gathered her stuff and ran to a car on the curb. "See you later!"

That is when I decided that it was definitely time to move.

Mother of the Year!

One of the most difficult things an adult can do is to tell their parents that they are gay. And, God bless and love my dad, he came through like a champ.

One of the first things he said was, "Son, do you want me to join some kind of support group?"

That's my dad!

Telling my mother I was gay was one of the weirdest experiences of my life.

A few of you have heard me tell stories about my mother. There are many words I could use to describe her:

Bipolar.

Unbalanced.

Peculiar.

There are other words I could use:

Weird.

Wanton.

Entrancing.

Criminal.

Or my favorite:

GODJIRA!

I had lived in fear of disappointing her as a kid. One word from her could crush my world. Utterly.

As I grew older and she grew weirder, I learned that her beloved younger brother was gay. He was such a disappointment to her. She would lean back with her wrist on her forehead, loudly moaning "WHYYYYY?" Seriously, can you imagine anything else that you would rather tell this woman than that her son was gay?

So, I didn't.

My mother made it easy as her life just got stranger and stranger. Alcohol led to Valium led to pot led to rumors led to unexplained deaths led to...you get the idea.

I confess to keeping my distance as my own life had absurd adventures enough. Why would I want to add more?

The last time I visited her during college I found her in the modern-day equivalent of an opium den and married to a man two years younger than I am. Spending three days with her new husband continually describing all the new, pretty colors he was seeing with pupils the size of pinheads convinced me that I had done my penance and was getting out.

****

Five Years Later

****

"Micheal, have you been drinking?"

"Yeah, Larr, I guess I havvvvvve."

"Why are you completely drunk off your ass on a Thursday night?" ask Larry.

"He duuuuuummmmped meeeeeee! WAAAAAAAAAAAAAAAH!"

"Who?" he asked.

"CARL DUMPED ME!!! SNIFFLE! BAWL! WAHHHHHHHHH!" I snuffled.

Larry looked around to make sure no one else was watching. He patted me on the shoulder.

"Did he say why?"

"You know how he wanted to move in together and how I found usssss a place?"

"Yes. Nice place." he answered.

"I asked him when he was going to move in and he said he wasn't. In fact, he had just renewed his lease! WAAAAAAAHHHH!"

"That fucker." hissed Larry.

"Yeah but he was MY fucker! SOOOOOOOOOOOBBBB!"

And so, it went on all night. I got gradually drunker and Larry fended off the horny prowlers. Eventually, he carried me home and poured me into bed.

****

The Next Morning

****

RING!!!

Wahhhh? HMMMM?

RING!!!

Oh, God! My HEAD!!!

RING!!!

Have you ever had a hangover so bad that you can hear your eyeballs move???

I have now.

RING!!!

WHY WAS THE SUN SO BRIGHT??? I swear that I could see sound.

I grabbed the phone only to hear a dial tone. The caller had hung up. Dragging myself into the bathroom, I looked into the mirror and barely recognized the face in front of me. I had slept on one side so my face looked half melted. My eyes had deep hollows under them and my skin had a faint greenish cast. My stomach felt as though I had eaten kittens and they were ready to erupt.

RING!!!

The goddamn phone began to ring again.

RING!!!

Moaning, I grabbed it.

"Hello, Micheal."

It was my mother! Why the hell did I pick up the phone?

"Hello."

"How you been?"

"Fine." I snapped. Not really but you know how it is.

"How's your father?"

"He's fine."

"How is your sister?"

"She's fine." I quickly answered looking for any excuse to get off the phone.

"You working?"

"Yes."

"Where?"

"A bank." again I grasped at some way to get off the phone.

"Who are you seeing?"

"No one." Wrong question.

"Why not?"

"Just no one. OKAY?"

"Why you being so goddamn surly?" she whined.

That did it!

"Because, Mother, I have just broken up with the person I have been seeing and I am not really in the mood to talk to anyone right now."

…especially YOU!

"Well, what was her goddamn name?" she demanded.

"Carl."

"What?"

"Mother...HIS name was CARL!" I spit out.

Two full minutes of silence followed.

"Mother?"

Nothing.

"Goodbye, Mother."

I hung up. Then I started to puke my guts out.

She didn't call back for 15 years.

The Law of Diminishing Returns

Sometimes expectations get ahead of you.

So, I had been dumped and was a blubbering basket case. To say that I was self-pitying and woe-is-me is to be mild. I dragged myself around like I was the only person in the world who had ever had their heart broken.

"Would you please stop all of that whining?" asked Larry.

"But, Larry – "

"Micheal, it has been a month. It is time to move along." He waved around the bar. "There are plenty of quirks in the gene pool."

It was a crowded Saturday night and we were watching the parade at the Tradewinds. The circuit consisted of an hour or so at the Garage then an hour at the Eagle. Then, if you didn't find what you were looking for, the Tradewinds. The A-listers might talk trash about the Tradewinds but even they had trouble getting laid at times.

Men wandered by in all shapes and sizes. All of them were looking for someone but they weren't quite sure who. Fat men. Thin men. Even men with spots. Short men. Tall men. Even men with chickenpox. Ooops, sorry...an old commercial for Armour Hot Dogs started running through my mind.

The air was thick with the smell of WAY too much cologne. Brut gave way to Cool Water to Fahrenheit to Aqua Velva. Separately, I am sure they smelled wonderfully but together they just plain stunk. You could have cut the air with a knife, squeezed it and bottled it and still have enough miasma left over for a ninth grader's sneakers.

Theodore came by and Larry wandered off with him leaving me leaning against a wall drinking my (fifth?) beer. That is when I decided that "Screw it! Larry is right!". I can't sit there and just feel sorry for myself.

I was gonna get laid, dammit!

But who was gonna be the lucky guy?

That is when I realized that I was surrounded by a bunch of dogs so bad they practically had fleas. It wasn't that they were old or ugly. It was that they were old AND ugly. I swear the Hunchback of Notre Dame was trying to cruise me that night.

Why, when I was actually looking to get laid, was I surrounded by bad toupees and dentures! I would not have been surprised to see a few men ambling by with walkers for support.

I was sliding into another alcohol haze when a shadow fell over me.

"Hey." rumbled down at me.

Looking up and up and further up, I realized I was standing next to a giant.

A hand the size of a small Chevy came my way.

"I'm Matt." he said while hopefully returning my hand.

"Mike."

Matt was enormous. Tall with muscles to match. Chest hair sprouted from his flannel shirt and the jeans had to have been painted on they were so tight. Cowboy boots on his feet and a hat to match. Whoa!

"Well, Mike, what did you say we get out of here?"

"You work fast." I said looking up.

"Is there really anyone here keeping you?" he smiled and gestured around the room.

"Good point." I finished my beer.

Before I knew it, we were back at his place.

He went to take a shower and I climbed into bed. This was going to happen. I was going to get laid!

Matt came out of the bathroom in a towel and dimmed the lights. Music began to play as he went around the room lighting candles. It was some bodice ripping novel come to life.

Eventually, he slid under the blankets and slyly tossed away the towel. It was shame really as I wanted to see him in all of his naked glory so to speak.

Lying beside of him, I felt like a minnow next to Moby Dick. He lay on his stomach making out. Things started to get hot and heavy. He turned over and my hand moved in and---

Nothing.

Seriously, nothing.

I couldn't find it.

It.

You know.

His tallywhacker.

His schlong.

His penis.

It just wasn't there.

At a total loss, I waited for him to move some more. But, no matter how he moved I couldn't see it in that dim light. It was like I was playing "Where's Waldo?" but Waldo just wasn't there.

I rolled over and his thigh brushed me.

"Oh, yeah, Baby." he moaned.

That is when I saw it. The only reason I knew it was his penis was because it was in the right place.

"Small" is being veeeeeeeery generous. "Tiny" is just too big.

"Microscopic" might work.

The man's Johnson resembled a tiny, pickled mushroom. It was quite literally the size of the tip of my little finger.

Karma, you are a bitch!

That is when it was time to leave. I rolled over one more time to get out of bed, accidentally brushed his thigh, and---

Matt was done!

Yup, just like that.

I was OOOOOUUUUUT of there!

Telling Larry the story later, he laughed.

"Only you can make a molehill out of a mountain, Micheal. Only you."

Mike Gets A Stalker!

When I tell people I had a stalker back in the '80's, they immediately think of movies like 'Friday the 13th" or "Halloween" where the killers chase teenagers through a forest with a knife.

Or Leatherface from the "Texas Chainsaw Massacre" cutting off peoples' faces to wear when he felt like a night on the town.

Not me.

When I think of my stalker, eight-inch stilettos and flaming red hair come to mind. Yup, my stalker was a transvestite. But that doesn't even begin to tell the story.

Let me correct myself. Let's use the term "sexually uncertain". Or maybe " clothing challenged". How about fucking weird?

Anyway, as I was slipping into my normal Saturday night alcohol induced haze, I leaned against the wall at the Garage and watching people go by. The night was especially grotesque with the Madonna and the Flock of Seagull wannabes competing with the normal crowd for attention.

Just as I was getting ready to head to the Eagle, up he came. Blocking my path was a slender "vision" in a purple, lilac patterned jumpsuit that looked more at home at Sunnyside Acres than a gay bar. Skinny and in high, high heels, the man teetered along at a towering five foot something. Fire engine red hair and beard and - what is it with the pink feathered boas?

I tried to slip past him on my way to the door. A hand grabbed my shoulder and I turned.

"Hello?" I said.

"Hallooed!" the man said in what I assume was supposed to be a seductive purr.

I stood there quietly. He seemed nonplussed at my lack of being overwhelmed.

"Well, nice to meet you!" I waved and swung out the door on the way to the Eagle.

The Eagle was no model forum that night either. They might play the best dance mix in the city, but you can only watch 20 lbs. of dough jiggling in a 2 lbs. flour sack for so long before queasiness sets in. After two more vodkas, it was time for the Tradewinds.

"Hello, again..." came from my left along with a cloud of "Charly" perfume. It was back. And blocking my way.

"I don't think we have been formally introduced. I'm Joseph!" He extended a wilting hand.

"And I am late meeting friends at the TW..." I said as I caught a gap in the parade and wandered out.

Three more vodkas later, the men at the Tradewinds weren't getting no purdier. Halloween had definitely come early.

"Don't You Want Me?" by the Human League had just started up when I decided that contrary to the song's title that "No!" I really did not want any of the people walking by.

I had walked to the bar as I did not want a DUI and was heading across the parking lot when an honest to god pink Cadillac pulled up beside me.

"Need a ride?"

It was him.

"No, thanks. The night air will do me good." I strode off.

After that every two or three blocks, the Caddy would slide up to the curb and yet another offer would be made and again refused.

Finally, I turned to the car as it slid up to the curve.

"Look, this is creepy. Stop following me!"

"Are you sure I can't give you a ride?" he pouted.

"I am going to be nice. You are NOT my type. Please leave me alone." I gritted.

"Can I at least buy you a drink sometime?" He asked.

"Sure. Now, go away!"

"Great!" With a triumphant smile, Joseph drove off.

Relieved, I trudged home and flopped into bed unaware that that my nightmare had just begun.

****

BANGBANGBANGBANGBANGBANG!!!

Who the hell was knocking on the apartment door? Rolling over, the clock said 8 am. Who was knocking at 8 A.M. on a Sunday morning?

Three guesses.

"Good morning!" said Joseph as he wound past me when I cracked the door open.

"What are you doing here?" I yawned.

"You said I could buy you a drink so here it is." He displayed a gallon of orange juice. "And I brought breakfast!" A dozen doughnuts waved my way.

"How the hell did you find out where I lived?"

"I followed you, of course." He smiled. "By the way, officially, I am Joseph Spooner."

"Mike Hobbs." I shook his limp hand. "Do you have any idea how weird this is?"

"Pshaw! I am sure you have had worse in your apartment on a Sunday morning." he laughed.

While it was true, it didn't make my mood any better.

Trying to be nice, I said, "I really need to be getting cleaned up and out as I am meeting friends." Which was actually true.

"Where are we meeting them?"

"WE are not meeting anyone. I am meeting some friends out."

Big-eyed, he said, "Oh, I see." Grabbing his purse, he headed to the door. "I've left my number on the counter. Call me for that drink."

Sighing in relief, I took a shower and cleaned up. Throwing on some clean clothes I headed out to meet Larry.

There used to be a restaurant on North High Street in Columbus called the Toll House. The food was decent, but the manager was a letch so we all called it the Troll House. It took a while to find a parking spot, but Larry had grabbed an outside table and was waiting.

"Micheal, you look like hell. Are you hungover?"

I began to tell Larry about my evening and why I was so tired when - "Oh, there you are!"

Guess who? Yup. Joseph.

He had changed into a lime green pantsuit with a large cream hat and sunglasses.

"Joseph? What are you doing here?"

"You promised me a drink. Remember?" and he sat down before I could stop him.

As Joseph introduced himself to Larry, he prattled on and on and on. Talking about his investments and his houses in Florida and his cars and money and his hobbies and his clothes and blah blah blah de blah. Larry and I just both sort of glazed over after a while.

Finally, Joseph went to the restroom. That is when Larry began to chuckle and then laugh out loud.

"Micheal, I have no idea why this one latched on to you, but you have got to get rid of him."

"I know but how? It followed me home!"

"Let me try." said Larry as Joseph came back to the table.

"Joseph, it has been delightful to meet you but Micheal has promised me that he would help me in my planting beds today. It's azalea time, you know!"

"It is?" said the weird one.

"Oh, yes and he is going to be there all day. We must be off."

With that, he swept me out of the restaurant and to his car.

"Thank you, Larry."

"Don't mention it but if he comes back around, make sure to have a bucket of water to throw on him." and he was off.

****

Monday was the next day and started badly. I couldn't find my work ID and had to wait for the security office to make me a new one. Otherwise, work went by quickly.

When you work in a call center with 2,000 other people all jammed at desks in one huge room, you tend not to notice the world around you. Finally, it was time to go home.

Walking up to my door, the first thing that I noticed was the huge bouquet of azaleas.

Oh, Shit!

"Meeting you was FATE!" said the card.

Entering my apartment, I looked around and thought I had walked in the wrong apartment. Someone had broken in and taken my stuff! All of my pictures and pillows and blankets were missing. Anything that could be moved had been removed...

And replaced with Holly Hobby and Strawberry Shortcake shit. Posters and throws and rugs and towels and anything else that could be had been taken and replaced with pictures of smiling dolls with enormous pink smiles and country kitchen crapola. It was everywhere. Except right above my bed.

In that spot of honor was an enormous framed photo of Joseph in full pantsuited and bearded glory.

Then the phone began to ring.

"Hello?"

"Hello, is this Mike Hobbs?"

"Yes, this is Paul Oliver with Mid-Ohio RV's."

"I think you have the wrong number."

"No, this is the number Mr. Spooner left. He asked me to call you and arrange for you to take delivery of your new motorhome."

"My motorhome?"

"Yes, Mr. Spooner said that as an employee of his company, he would put down the down payment, but you would be responsible for the other payments."

Deep breath. And another.

"Mr. Oliver? I am afraid that I have left Mr. Spooner's employment as of a few hours ago and will not be taking delivery of the unit. Please contact Mr. Spooner directly for further instructions. Thank you."

I hung up.

Searching my apartment, I found all of my stuff hidden in the shower and the closets. I piled all of the kitschy crapola in a big pile on the living room floor as I put my own stuff back.

Again, the phone rang.

"Micheal! I had expected to hear from you earlier."

"Joseph, how did you get the hell into my apartment?" I demanded.

"That sounds hardly grateful."

"For what? For breaking into my apartment? For bringing all this crap into my place?"

"If you didn't want people stopping in to redecorate, then you need to stop leaving an emergency key under the mat."

I hung up and spent the rest of the evening changing the locks.

****

Tuesday, my workday started well even if I had to get a temporary ID as I must have misplaced my badge. Things were cruising along when my phone rang.

"Mike?"

"Yeah?"

"This is Carol at the front desk. Could you come out here for a second?"

"Sure."

Mildly curious, I walked all the way across the giant room and into the front lobby.

There was Joseph. He was standing between two security guards. More important, he was dressed exactly the same as I was. Same shirt, same pants, same shoes. He even had a pair of glasses on that looked like mine.

"What the hell is going on?" I blurted out.

"We found your missing ID." said Carol the receptionist.

Joseph hung his head in shame. "I just wanted to see you." he said.

"Should we have him arrested?" asked Carol.

"No, just please get him out of my sight." I answered and headed back to my desk. My boss, Loretta, and I had a good laugh about it.

Hoping that was the end of it, I worked for several more hours.

Midafternoon, I had gotten back into my stride.

As I have said, working in a room with 2,000 people you tend not to notice noise as it all dulls to a slow buzz. It is when the buzz stops that you become aware that something unusual is going on.

Sensing a disturbance in the Force, I looked up. Everyone seemed to be looking to the entrance. One of the guards had just come through the door and was carrying something large. It looked like a flower arrangement of some type. He was so far away that I couldn't see it well and wondered who was getting flowers.

My heart skipped a beat as I finally got a good look at it and realized it was coming my way.

"Loretta! You have no idea where I am! Send it to a conference room for God's sake!" and dived below my desk. I stayed there trying to breathe quietly.

Loretta chuckled as the guard came up. I heard her ask the guard to take the flowers to a small conference room nearby. I crouched and waited.

"The coast is clear." I heard her whisper.

I climbed out and stretched.

"Now, what exactly is going on, Mike?" Loretta asked as we walked towards the conference room.

"You wouldn't believe me if I told you."

The arrangement was truly hideous. It was a horseshoe shaped funeral arrangement that was taller than I. Made of hundreds of heart-shaped pink roses it bore a pink satin banner that read "I'm Sorry!". That was what had been carried through my office.

As I told her what had happened, Loretta began to chuckle. By the time I was done, she was breathless.

"Tell you what," she said, "let's make lemonade out of lemons."

That night, every woman heading home was given a pink rose as she left. Larry met me at the house and I filled him in. Larry had also done his research and found out that Joseph was a penniless conman who lived off his grandmother's pension.

"Oh, Micheal...." he said in a tired voice.

"Larr, I just don't know what to do."

"Did you call the police?"

"They said because nothing was missing there was nothing there was nothing they could do. As a matter of fact, they had never heard of a burglar LEAVING new items. Then, they laughed."

"Only you."

The phone rang.

"Did you get my flowers?" chimed Joseph.

"Yes, I got them. Now, leave me alone!" I slammed down the phone.

The phone immediately began to ring again.

"Let me handle this." began Larry as he reached for the receiver. He cleared his throat to lower it.

"Hello? ... No, this isn't Mike. This is his boyfriend, John." Larry drawled as deeply as he could. "Let me end this right now.... Listen, carefully.... If you so much as bother my boyfriend again, I will rip your head off and shit down your throat...Yeah, shit down your throat...Is that clear? Good." He hung up.

Larry took a sip of his wine and smiled.

After five minutes, the phone began to ring. This time, I picked it up.

"Hello?"

"So, what does this mean for us?" demanded Joseph.

"Us? Get this straight. There is no us! There has never been and US! THERE NEVER WILL BE AN US!!! IS THAT CLEAR?" Silence. "John would like to speak with you."

Joseph hung up.

It was over...

****

Or so I thought.

TEN YEARS LATER

I was getting a chance to take a vacation in Key West and was staying at the Island House. I pulled on some trunks and sidled down to the pool. Diving in, I came up for air and heard a gasp. Running away in high heels and a silk robe was Joseph.

I yelled out "John, look! It's Joseph!" and the figure ran faster.

I later heard he checked out early.

The Bonfire of the Vanities?

It absolutely amazes me how shallow gay men can be at times and they were the same during the 1980's.

Let me give you an example:

I have never been an A-Lister and I never will be.

I have no sense of style. Seriously, I have the clothing sense of a dead lizard. I could take a Dolce and Gabbana tux and make it look like an old dishtowel.

So how did I end up at the party of the year?

Food poisoning, that's how.

THE A list couple in Columbus, Daniel and Robert (pronounced Roh-Bare) had descended from Olympus and had announced that they were holding a fundraiser for those less fortunate. They were going to have a huge party at the Garage and all proceeds would go to a fledgling AIDS group.

Anyone who was ANYONE was invited.

And the theme was going to be Gods and Goddesses.

The hosts needed an excuse to wear as little as possible and to display the wings we all knew they really had.

The newspaper needed someone to cover the party, but the original person assigned had eaten at a new "trendy" restaurant that would NOT be getting a good review if the sounds of him barfing on the other side of the telephone line were anything to judge by. He had gone down the roster and everyone was busy except me. You could hear the hesitancy in his voice.

"Just don't do anything embarrassing and it will be fine." he said. "Oh, and you have to dress up."

Oh, great...

My salvation answered the phone on the first ring.

"Yes, Micheal. I have some old costumes here that you can borrow." said Larry. "As a matter of fact, why don't you drop over about 6 and we can pick out something for you and we can go together."

"Together?"

"You can bring someone, right?"

"Oh, yes."

"Do you think that I am going to miss the party of the year?" he asked.

That is how I ended up at the Garage dressed as Hermes, winged cap and all. Fake clouds, fog machines and strobing lights were supposed to let everyone know that Olympus had descended to Earth. Fake Trojans wandered around with trays handing out Trojans (condoms, that is) and the drinks certainly were strong.

Larry being Larry was immediately surrounded by a throng and I just tried to stay in the background. My winged boots itched, and the loincloth kept threatening to slide off at any moment. And this damn safety pin kept coming loose and jabbing me at inopportune times. Anyone watching must have thought I had fleas or something.

The costumes were amazing. And the guests seemed to have chosen the ones that allowed them to show the most skin. Dueling Achilles with drooping plastic spears circled each other while twin Venus drag queens did their best to outvamp each other. Pumped biceps and fake breasts were the theme for the evening.

One man wandered through and was getting all sorts of odd looks. He was dressed in what appeared to be rags and a crutch. A taller man - he even had a cloth wrapped around his eyes (although from the way he was walking about, it was clear he could see plain as day.

"Pardon me, but who are you supposed to be?" I asked.

"I am the Oracle of Delphi. I can see the futures of men. Would you like to see your own?" he whispered and reached for my hand.

"Sure."

"You must ask it as a question." he continued.

"Will I find someone?" I asked.

Staring at my hand, he leaned in and said "Oh, yes. But more important, you will survive the coming dark."

"Dark?" but he released my hand and wandered off without another word.

Mystified, I watched the party for a while longer. The salons and the waxing parlors had certainly done a brisk business that day.

Suddenly, a hand the size of small ham landed on my shoulder. Turning, I was confronted with Hercules, quite literally.

"Are you from the gay newspaper?" he asked.

"Yes."

"Daniel and Robert would like to see you."

Dutifully, I followed him to the private area of the club. The hosts were holding court dressed as Ra and Isis. The guards were certainly muscular and wearing just enough to make this a PG-Rated party.

"Are you enjoying yourself?" asked Daniel from behind a kohl-lined eye.

"Very much so."

"Anything to help the community." he answered while turning to a tray of stuffed olives.

"Where are the people who the fundraiser is for?" I asked.

Cold silence.

"We will see them tomorrow." said Robert within his wig. "There is no reason for sick people to be here."

"But wouldn't it help raise money if people knew who they were helping?"

"Darling, this party is for the healthy among us to help those who need. Why embarrass them?" a discomfited Daniel asked.

"Just make sure we are on the front page. That should help raise awareness." said Robert.

After that, the interview was clearly over, and I was escorted out of the VIP area.

Larry was holding court as normal near the bar and I decided another drink was in order. The party was in high gear and the music was loud. The entire bar was jumping.

Then, "I Will Survive" by Gloria Gaynor started up.

My back was to the dance floor, but I heard the hubbub slowly die and turned to find the reason. It took me a minute but then I noticed that the dancers had stopped. They all appeared to be staring at one man.

The Oracle of Delphi was in the middle of the dance floor and dancing away for all he was worth. He was twirling that crutch over his head and moving as though he was made for music. He was also slowly stripping and that is why all the dancers were watching.

As the Oracle shed more clothing, bluish lesions began to appear as his skin was uncovered. Bandages and bruises from IV's covered his arms. Although tall, he was clearly ill and very thin.

A huge smile covered the dancer's face as the song went on. He was clearly having the time of his life.

"Oh, my God. He's got AIDS." someone whispered nearby.

The entire bar was entranced and watching every move. All other activity stopped.

Finally, the song climaxed, and the Oracle twirled the crutch around his head and slammed it down on the dance floor. Breathing hard, he looked around at the growing silence.

In the hush, a figure walked in from the side of the dance floor and up to him.

"Honey, you look like you could use a drink." said Larry.

Placing his arm around him, they walked off the dance floor and we three exited the party with a smile.

The Wrong Bed....

Have I got a story...

People ask me how I met my friend Beth and when they do we look at each other and smile knowingly.

"We met through friends back in '87" is how we both answer.

The truth is a little more complex.

****

SLAM!

"Hmmmph? Wha?"

The bed jumped as someone hopped out.

"Shit!"

Everything went dark as a blanket was thrown over my head.

"Hmm?"

"SHHHHH! It's my wife!" came a harsh whisper

"Wife?"

"Just QUIET!!!!" came back. "Stay here."

How the hell did this happen you may ask?

Well, the previous night I was sitting at the Garage watching the parade go by and bored out of my mind. The vodka was not helping, and I was going slowly insane. Larry was tired and had stayed in so I was alone.

"Has anyone told you that you look just like Jim Carrey?" came over my shoulder.

There have been worse pickup lines. A few:

"You know you look just like my Dad?"

"Is this where the angels meet?"

Even "I just got tested. No herpes. Guaranteed!"

So, I gave him the benefit of the doubt.

"No, can't say they have. Mike." I put out my hand.

"Jerry." he said shaking my hand.

He was cute. Very cute actually. We started to talk and started to get late. His roommate was out of town visiting his mother. One thing led to another and...

So, there I was hidden under a blanket and listening. I could hear voices mumbling from downstairs but could not make out what they were saying. Finally, I heard a door shut and then a car drove off.

Relieved, I started to breathe easier.

"Hello?" a woman's voice came from the hallway.

Bolt upright, I grabbed my pants and ran for the closet. Hopping, I tried to pull on my pants and fell flat on my face. Leaping to my feet, I closed the door behind me and tried to breathe easier.

I heard the bedroom door open.

"Hello?"

Breathe. Breathe. Breathe.

The door to the closet opened.

"There you are!" said the smiling redhead who opened the door. "Aren't you a bit tired of closets?"

I smiled sheepishly.

"Ummm..."

"I'm Beth. Come out of there. It's okay."

"Ummm..." I mumbled.

"I swear I don't bite."

Exiting the closet, I started to get dressed. Beth continued chattering away.

"I sent Jerry to the store for orange juice. We're out. Are you hungry?"

"Yeah."

"Come on downstairs. I'm making eggs. Do you want some?" she continued as she led me downstairs. The kitchen was nice.

"Again, I am Beth."

"I'm Mike." I said sitting.

"How do you like your eggs, Mike?"

"Over easy."

"Deal."

"I have to ask this: doesn't this make you uncomfortable?" I queried.

"What? That my husband is gay? Hah! I've known for years."

"You have?"

"Oh, yeah. Once I figured he knew more about color swatches than I did, I could see what side of the toast his bread was buttered on."

"And?" I asked.

"And, what?" she said laying a plate in front of me.

"What are you going to do about it?"

"Why should I do anything? I am perfectly happy the way things are." she waved her spatula.

"What about people like me?"

"Well, there are a few rules and one of those is that he doesn't bring people home." she smiled.

"Oh?" my eyebrows went up.

"So, he and I will be having a "little talk"." she air-quoted.

I was The Other Man!!!

Beth and I kept talking and talking. Cooking. Movies. Books. You name it.

Jerry came home with the orange juice. He looked at me with a look of "Please No!" on his face.

Beth spoke first.

"Bad Jerry! No Treat!"

"Arf?" he smiled closely.

Beth tapped his nose with a newspaper.

And that was it.

"Now, get this boy home." she ordered. "Oh, and Mike?"

"Yes?"

"Dinner next week?"

And that was it.

****

More than 25 years have passed since then. I just hung up the phone.

Beth never changes.

The Easter Bunny Cometh

"Have you lost your mind?" said Larry.

"Please, Larr. I have a hangover."

"And why would that be?" He gave me the eye.

"I was out at the Eagle last night-"

"Of course, you were..."

"Please, Larr. So anyway, everyone was talking about how the owners were sponsoring this contest."

"Is that Mr. Midwest?"

"Yeah. So, anyway, I was sitting there drinking when Jack and Tom, the owners came up and started chatting me up. They knew I worked for "Gay Times" and asked me if someone from the paper was covering the contest. I told them I was."

"How did you end up with this?" Larry asked holding up a card with a number written on it.

"Well, they asked me if I wanted backstage access and, of course, I did. Then, we all started doing rounds of shots and they began to tell me that they didn't have enough contestants and, before I knew it-"

"You volunteered?"

"Yup."

"On the night before Easter Sunday..."

"I think the Lord will forgive me, Larry."

"Oh, Myyyy."

"Don't give me that tone. I need help."

"You seem to be doing well on your own as it is." Larry snarked.

"Please, Larry. What am I gonna do?"

"You could always not show up."

"I can't. I promised." I whined.

"While drunk."

"As a skunk, but a promise is a promise." I sighed. "I would never be able to show my face in there again."

"A loss the size of the Titanic..." He truly was a master of sarcasm.

"Seriously..."

"Okay." Larry said accepting the inevitable. "What do you need help with?"

∙∙∙

Twelve hours later.

"You know you can still back out." whispered Larry.

"I wish." Sigh. "Here goes nothing."

I stepped out into the maelstrom. Turns out only three actual contestants showed up. Besides me, there was a tall Hispanic queen dressed in TIGHT jeans and a silk shirt and a short college kid who was furry enough for Teddy Ruxpin. There we stood flanked by giant blowup Easter bunnies. Oh, and the contest was fixed. I had heard through the grapevine that the kid was the "special friend" of one of the bar owners. At least, I could only end up getting third place.

There I was in my geekish, awkward way dressed in my best bar outfit. This consisted of jeans shorts, half boots and a T-shirt that said "Hello, Sailor!" on it. A Coors ball cap topped it all off.

Bubbles, the emcee, was this huge, tipsy, drag queen who seemed to have more hands than an octopus. She was also dressed like Julie Andrews in the " Sound of Music" except that she was wearing a huge pair of bunny ears instead of a wimple.

We all got called out on stage and introduced. Then, Bubbles insisted on stripping us of our shirts to catcalls from the audience.

"Contestant number one is Raoul. Raoul is a hair dresser who wants to work with at risk youth -"

"I bet he does!" came out of the crowd.

Bubbles looked around. 'Now, Honey, try not to interrupt Mama here. She hasn't taken her Valium tonight and you know how she gets."

Laughter went up.

"Contestant number two is Teddy. Teddy is studying Human Sexuality at OSU -"

"And in the alley behind the bar!" interrupted the heckler.

Bubbles gave the crowd the stink eye.

"Now, Darling, Mama is getting irritated and you do NOT want to see her mad!" She again glared but no response.

"Finally, we have Mike." She stopped and glared. "Mike is a bill collector..." she looked around. " and he knows where you live!" Even I gulped at that.

After a rounded of applause, it was time for the talent contest.

Raoul went first. He "danced". A better term was he attempted to move every part of his body in different directions at the same time to a disco beat. He reminded me of a bowl of jello fantasia with epilepsy. It was just a miracle no one's eye was put out.

Next was Teddy. And he started to "sing" and he was godawful. Nails on a chalk board can keep a better tune. The only thing louder than his screeching was the sound of the beer bottles cracking as his notes hit heretofore unknown sharps.

BUT there was worse. He took my song! He sang "Tomorrow" from "Annie" and I had nothing left to perform and no music!

"Larry! He took my song! What do I do?"

"What is that annoying thing you always hum in the shop?"

"Really?!?"

"Do you have much choice?"

"And, now let's bring to the stage Contestant Number Three..." started up Bubbles. "...Mike!"

And suddenly there I was in the middle of that stage with every eye on me.

Larry waved at me to start.

It was the only song I knew right then and there.

"Well, life on the farm is kinda laid back
Ain't much an old country boy like me can't hack
It's early to rise and early in the sack
Thank God, I'm a country boy"

Smiling, the whole bar joined in, clapping and singing. Until one final huge choir of "Thank God, I'm A Country Boy" rang out to end it.

Phewww!!!

"Weeeeeell. Wasn't that just special?" asked Bubbles as the applause ended. The contestants exited the stage as Bubbles began her performance. Why is it that every drag queen insists on performing "I'm Every Woman." by Chaka Khan?

In the dressing room, we slammed shots of Tequila and dressed (or should I say undressed?) for the last part of the contest. We all stripped down to our underwear and drank heavily.

"Oh, slight change of plans. Put these on!" shouted the bar owner as he handed us bunny ears.

"Wha?" I began.

"No time. You're on!" he said as he pushed us out.

"Let's welcome back to the stage our contestants, Raoul, Teddy and Mike!" shouted Bubbles as we bounded out looking like Playboy bunnies gone bad. They were supposed to ask us some question on the events of the day and then the whole thing would be over. My answer to whatever question was going to be "World Peace" so I was ready.

"And now," began Bubbles. World Peace. "we are ready for the final part of our contest." World Peace. "All of our contestants" World Peace. "are going to" World Peace. "dance for you." World Pe-

WHAT?

DANCE???

ME?

I don't know if any of you have seen me dance but I have all the grace of a flamingo caught in a blender. There is no one I know who would ever call me graceful. And now I had to dance?

"Now, boys, as this is Easter. I want you to take one of these baskets and dance among these fine bar patrons and collect plastics eggs from them. They are supposed to be putting donations inside of each of them."

World Peace?

And the music started.

I tried to move my way through the crowd to the music, but it was close quarters. My basket slowly filled as I tried to get done as quickly as possible. That is when I felt someone slipping a couple of the eggs down the front of my tighty whiteys and they tried to cop a feel. Batting their hand away, I lurched over to where Larry stood with drink in hand.

"Michael, please take those eggs out of your shorts now."

"I will in a second."

"Do it now."

"Why?" I asked.

"Because it looks like you have four testicles." he replied.

And he was right. I pulled them out as quickly as I could and made my way back to the stage.

Teddy, the young kid, and the anointed but as yet uncrowned winner, was already there and Bubbles was counting his eggs.

"Ten." she shouted to polite applause.

She counted mine.

"Seventeen." she shouted.

"Raoul, where are you?" she said as she looked for the last contestant.

That is when we caught sight of Raoul. I am not quite sure how to describe the dance that he was doing but it drew the eye. Maybe "Bunny Hop" meets "Disco Inferno"? However, what really drew the eye was the fact that he had discarded the basket that he was carrying in favor of another collection method.

Raoul was putting all the eggs down the front of his pants. He looked as though he had eight or nine pulsating, shifting testicles. It reminded me of that scene from "Alien" when the egg is about to burst. But, that was far from the worst part of his performance.

As Raoul jiggled, shook and seizured, most of the eggs had shifted from the front of his underwear to the back without him noticing drunk as he was. He now sported a good 20 or so eggs in the rear panel. The poor man looked as though Baby had gone boom-boom in the dipey-poo.

It was simply hypnotic.

After that, the rest of the contest went by in a blur.

Oh, I got second.

Freddy Mercury Is A God!!!

There really is a God.

And his name is Freddy Mercury.

Coming out in the Hair Metal Age and the Material Girl years meant I always had a skewed idea about music. Seriously, I was so naïve that I never knew what some of the biggest hits of the decade were actually about.

Heck, I even thought "Relax" was about RELAXING!

Let's try a few:

"Y.M.C.A." by the Village People

Well, DUH!

"I'm Coming Out" by Diana Ross

Sure, I could understand how the title might be equated with gay pride, but I really thought it had to do with going out to party.

Imagine how surprised when I found out that it was written after the writer visited a club for transvestites. Supposedly while waiting to pee, he saw three different Diana Rosses waiting in line for the urinal as well.

"One Night in Bangkok" by Murray Head

I thought that this was about chess, for heaven's sake. It wasn't until much later that I heard the rumors about Thailand's capital and its ability to appeal to every proclivity from underage to senior sex. And, with the song being about voyeurism, it was so far out of my experience range that the true meaning went soaring right over my head.

"She Bop" by Cyndi Lauper

Talk about naïve!

It may be stereotyped but as a gay man I had never thought about a woman playing with herself. I am a guy, after all, and adolescent boys are notorious for doing things with the doors closed later at night but a GIRL? EWWWWWWWWWWWW! I was simply appalled when I found out the true meaning of the song.

It still makes me blush.

"Turning Japanese" by The Vapors

Completely flummoxed by this one. I just went with the flow. Many years later, I found out it is supposedly the look on your face when you orgasm. Never thought about it before but don't we all close our eyes at THAT moment?

"Safety Dance" by Men Without Hats

I was absolutely sure this WAS about safe sex! Everybody I knew thought so, too. How disappointing to find out it simply mean being able to slam dance without being arrested for it.

I still prefer my meaning.

"Karma Chameleon" by Culture Club

Fool that I am, I thought this was about the riverboat in the video. It was beautiful and just seemed perfect. How was I to know "You come and go." referred to the fact that the lead singer was having a secret affair with his (male) guitarist? It kind of ruins it.

AND OF COURSE:

"Relax" By Frankie Goes to Hollywood.

I honestly thought that this had to do with enjoying yourself at a party and just going with the flow. Reaaallllly! I did.

I mean I heard "Relax, when you wanna come." But zoned it in one ear and out the other.

I didn't know they made three videos for this. The one I always saw was a concert one that was definitely G Rated. It was not until much later that I saw the REAL video featuring the S & M flavored Roman orgy video. That was a real mindblower.

But, as a stated before, the true God of the 1980's was Freddy Mercury, the lead singer of Queen. Although he never admitted it publicly, everyone on the planet knew the man was gay. I mean a blind and deaf man would have known that fact from a distance of ten miles.

And, that is why I adored him utterly and completely.

"We Are The Champions"

THE ultimate song about screaming out that you are proud of who you are.

"We Will Rock You"

Stand up and be who you are. Be a real man.

"I Want To Break Free"

Who the hell cares what other people think about you as long as YOU are happy.

"Who Wants To Live Forever?"

Grab life by the balls and run with it as hard as you can because this is the only chance you are going to get!

And finally, my all-time favorite song:

"Bohemian Rhapsody"

Has there ever been a song recorded that more people shout out as loud as they can when it plays?

Who out there can honestly say they don't know every single word?

Even the biggest "he-man" I know slips into their highest falsetto squints and points to the sky to be sure they hit it at just the right spot. "For Me-e-e-e-e-e-e-e-e-e!!!!" I am surprised we don't see more shattered windshields from those off-key notes while driving.

The real magic of this song is the fact that every single person starts to sing when this plays. And, everyone breaks into the riff playing the magically appearing air guitar during the final bridge.

The song makes everyone one person.

One community.

One soul.

What else can I say?

This Is Not A Test!

Life is full of tests.

Spelling tests.

Math tests.

College entrance exams.

Skills tests for jobs.

Then, there are the tests that change your life.

Drivers' tests.

Cholesterol tests.

Even pregnancy tests.

I mean, think about it. Our life is made of tests.

You might even say that life itself is a huge test.

I remember taking THE test for the first time. You know the one I mean, right?

Nowadays, everyone is all nonchalant about it.

THE test. The one that could change your life.

The AIDS test?!?

These days it is the "HIV" test.

In the 1980's, no one called it that. It was always "The AIDS test". It was a wonderful yet terrifying thing.

Yes, I meant to say that.

"Wonderful" in that it finally gave us a way to find out who had been exposed to IT!

If positive, we could start making life decisions. Wills. Treatment where available. Estate planning.

If not, the sky was the limit.

"Terrifying" in that you could find out if you were going to live or die. Period. Treatment regimens had barely crawled out of the stone age and even when they worked you could die from the toxicity of the very drugs themselves.

AZT? What's that?

So, imagine you are nerdy, geeky, single boy who is afraid of everything and everyone when THE Test becomes available. What would you do?

Let me rephrase that: what if you were a geeky, insecure, paranoid man and it came around - then what would you do?

Get drunk and ignore it....right? Riiiiiiight!

So, I did for about a year.

It wasn't difficult. I mean it was expensive and hard to get to start out with. And I hated the idea of giving blood for any reason.

Then -

"Mike?"

"Tom?"

"Yeah, Mike. Need to talk to you about something."

Tom and I had dated for a couple weeks but I had gotten bored with his constant prattle. It was amicable.

"Mike, um, don't know to say this so I just am: You need to go get tested." he drawled.

"Don't tell me you have gonorrhea?" I asked.

"No, um, I just got, um, the, um, AIDS, um, test...and it came back positive."

HOLY FUCKING SHIT!!!!!

Paaaaaaauuuuuuuusssssseeeeeee.

"You still there, Mike?"

"Yeah, um, yeah."

"Figured I had to tell you."

Sigh.

"Well, thanks." I hung up.

OH, MY GOD!!!

FUUUUUUUUUUUUUUUUUUUUUUUUUUUUUUUUUUUUUUUUUUUUUUUUUUUUUUUUUUUUUUUUUUUUUUUUUUUUUUUUUUUUUUUUUUUUUIUUUUUUUUUUUUUUUUCCCCKKKKK!!!!!!!!!!!!!!

But I play safe....

Fuck!

Yes? No. Yes? No. Yes? No. Aaaaaaaaaaaarrrrrrrgggggghhhhh!!!!!

****

Three Days Later

....which is how I came to be sitting in the waiting room of the Free Clinic.

The room was designed to calm you down while you waited for whatever pronouncement of Doom awaited. Drab colors competed with colorful posters to make certain that you knew life was a gamble and you may have lost.

"Herpes and You?" said one.

"What is that Lump?" asked another.

"Your Friend, Your Prostate." reassured a third.

I had only been there for 10 minutes but was already climbing the walls. The room was half full of people all avoiding eye contact. We were all wondering why the others were there, but it was none of our damn business, thank you very much!

Of course, a couple were fairly obvious. The lady of the night wearing way too little clothing for a January morning was probably here for her twice weekly STD test. The gentleman with the bloody bandage and his left arm dangling probably really should have been at the ER. Et cetera.

Finally, I was called back and placed in a room to wait. And wait. And wait. I know it wasn't more than five minutes, but it seemed to stretch forever.

A nurse entered and check my vital signs. Then, she asked me to extend my arm. This was, honestly, the first time in my life I had ever voluntarily given blood. Tying off my arm, she tapped it.

"You have nice veins." she said.

What do you say to that?

"Thank you."

Moving swiftly, she gloved and took the sample. I watched as the vial filled. Then she tucked them in a sample box and removed the straps.

"Be back here in two weeks." she said turning away.

Yep, it took two weeks back then. None of the instant results we have now.

And I was shuttled out the door.

****

T W O

    W E E K S

        L A T E R

The period between taking the test and getting the results was the worst in my entire life. I did not eat for two weeks. I did not sleep for two weeks. I almost lost my job as I was so nervous for two weeks.

Two weeks is 14 days. Two weeks is 336 hours. Two weeks is 20,160 minutes. Two weeks is 1,209, 600 seconds.

And I felt every single second count down like some cosmic clock.

During those two weeks, I lost 15 lbs.

I converted to every religion on the planet and even invented a couple myself.

I examined my life to find out how I went wrong and promised to be the saint I should have been.

I felt the continents moving and even they moved faster than that two-week period.

****

Only to find myself back in the same dreary waiting room with most of the same people.

I was called back into an examining room and waited. I could not sit I was so nervous, so I just stood there in the corner trying to distract myself by reading hemorrhoid brochures. And, I had to pee like a racehorse.

After an eternity, the nurse entered with my file. Then, she locked the door. She locked the door! OHMIGOD!!! This is bad! THIS IS SO BAD!!! SHE LOCKED THE DOOR SHE LOCKED THE DOOR SHE LOCKED THE DOOR -

"Mr. Hobbs, I don't know what you have been doing or why you got tested-"

SHE LOCKED THE DOOR!!!

"-but you are negative!"

SHE LOCKED- Wha?

The room went black.

The next I knew, the nurse was trying to help me up off the floor where I had passed out and into a sitting position.

"I don't have it?"

"No, you don't." she said handing me a cup of water.

The "Our Father" prayer started running through my head. Stupid, I know, but it did.

I giggled. I actually giggled. The nurse looked at me and smiled.

"Mr. Hobbs, go home and get some sleep."

As I walked down the steps of that hidden little building, it really was a bunny and butterflies day. My feet were three feet off the pavement. I walked down to the bus stop like I owned the world.

I didn't have it.

That is when I realized that when I passed out I had peed myself.

Saint Mike?

"Micheal, what are you doing?"

"Hey, Larry. I am just adding up my life."

"What on earth for?"

"I looked Death in the eye, Larr, and do not like what I saw." I said looking up at him.

"Does this still have to do with that stupid test?"

"I am a bad, bad man, Larr."

"We are all sinners and saints, Micheal." He looked over my kitchen table.

"What are all these Post-its?"

"These are the bad things I have done over here..."

"In fuchsia?"

"I thought pink was appropriate. And the good things I have done over here in blue."

Larry picked one up.

"Fudged my resume?" He arched an eyebrow.

"I put my GPA as 3.2 and it was really 3.16."

"Horrors!" he mused picking up another. "I told someone I was allergic when I realized what a terrible cook they were."

"Yeah..."

"Wow! I am surprised it is not raining hellfire already."

He picked up a blue sheet.

"I gave my last dollar to a homeless guy. Hmm. Admirable but he probably bought beer."

"Be that as it may." I said. "It is the thought that counts."

"Why are these neon orange?"

"Those are the promises I am making."

"Six of these say, 'Stop Drinking'. Really?" Larry turned to me.

"Really..."

"Good!"

"Finish my book? Are you writing a book?"

"Yeah...sci-fi." I hedged.

"Any good?"

"Maybe..."

"So how is that a saintly act?" Larry queried.

"I may have been stretching a little."

"What are the yellow?"

I cleared my throat.

"Those are the questionable ones."

"Questionable?"

"You know. Stuff that I wasn't sure about."

Larry grabbed a couple.

"I always take the last slice of pizza." An eyebrow raised. "That is certainly pitchfork worthy there."

"Come on..."

"I like this one." A smile. "I Suck Dick." Chuckle.

"Larr-"

"I would put that in the Heavenly category myself."

"Ummm-"

"Along with buttfucking." He grinned. "If done right."

"Oh, come on."

"What is this one? 'Devote My Life to Charity'"

"Larry, I need to start thinking about other people."

My friend started to look around.

"Okay, where is it?"

"What?"

"I know it has to be here somewhere." he said as he peered into the broom closet. "Where did you put it?"

"Put what? What are you looking for?"

"The cross, of course!"

"Cross?"

"Isn't a crucifix THE accessory for a martyr, Micheal?"

"But, Larr -"

"Micheal, you listen here, and listen good! You are one of the nicest, most selfless people I know."

"But -"

"But nothing! You would give someone the coat off your back if you thought they needed it. Now, CUT THIS OUT AND STOP BEATING

YOURSELF UP BECAUSE YOU HAVE GOTTEN LUCKY WHERE OTHERS HAVEN'T!!!"

I opened my mouth to say something but -

"DO I MAKE MYSELF CLEAR?" He leaned over the table.

Deep breath.

"Yes, sir."

"Good." Larry smiled. "Now, you want to get a beer?"

Another deep breath.

"Sure."

"Oh," he purred, "and you're paying."

Nice Shoes...Wanna F*$#???

As the social changes of the 1980's accelerated, it became harder and harder to figure out your place in the world. It was like being on a playground merry-go-round that just kept going faster and faster and faster and...

Or better yet, musical chairs where the music is playing and then "Pop! Goes the --"! Quick! Sit down NOW!!!

You better damn well take that person right next to you home or you might not get that chance again!

Even people's behavior changed.

Picture it -

Gay Bar, 1987

Saturday night and the joint is packed.

Take a deep breath.

Again.

Seriously, take a real deep breath.

Smell that?

Yeah, that's right.

The smell is so thick you can almost taste it. That's the smell of desperation. It fills the sinuses and makes the eyes water.

Yeah. These people don't just want to get laid.

They NEED to get laid.

It affects their every behavior. It even came out in the way they introduced themselves.

That is how the "pickup line" came to be.

What is the worst pickup line that you have ever heard?

Now take down the level. Split it by half and then take away the top 90% and you have the typical gay bar pickup line from the 80's.

I have heard them all.

There were the mundane and common.

"Nice shoes...wanna fuck?"

Umm, no.

How about the blond who purred?

"You got any syrup?"

"No, why?

"Because I wanna eat you up."

Anyone got any insulin?

"Someone get me some ice because it just got HOT in here!" said the effeminate young man with too much eye makeup and a silk boa as he eyed me up and down.

Just...no.

The glittery, mulleted young one who drunkenly giggled as he talked.

"Heaven must be listening because an angel just walked in!"

Barkeep! Beer!

Another time, the short, dark man seemed to be staring at my mouth.

"That is some of the worst gingivitis I have ever seen outside of dental school. Want me to floss you?"

Or another time, a skinny young man in way too little leather and assless chaps grabbed my arm as I walked by.

"Nice wrists! Do you like Crisco?"

The mind boggles.

Or, how about Bubba over there?

"Ever had sex in a hog barn?"

Truly.

Even the creepy if cute young man in the corner as he ran a finger up my arm.

"You know, you kinda look like my Dad."

Ewwwwwwwwwwwwwwww!

But the very worst that I ever heard was one night in the Eagle. Pickings were slim and I was getting ready to go home when another young man came walking by one night. He was kind of cute.

The only problem was that he had a very strong chemical smell about him.

Really strong.

And his pickup line was certainly, um, unique.

"I can guarantee I don't have crabs."

So, that was the smell!

Aqua Velva mixed with RID!

Not quite ready for a crab boil, I was Outa There!

My night ended with me, a tub of butter pecan ice cream and a cat.

I considered it a win.

Waiting For The Ball To Drop

So, I got beat up by a drag queen...

New Year's Eve, 1987

The Garage was packed, and I was trying to get past everyone without spilling my drink. Yeah, I know a Bloody Mary is not meant to drink at night, but I figured why the hell not and talked the bartender into it.

Streamers flew and balloons filled the air as midnight approached. Drag queens and glitter flowed like candy.

I was winding my way past the dance floor when a drunk tripped me. My drink went flying.

Pickles McGee, grande dame of the evening, looked up from her splattered white chiffon with a look of Death in her eye. Her glare could have melted glass.

"I'll be glad to pay-" I started to sputter

WHAM! The room went dark!

I awoke lying on the floor with a furious Pickles standing over me shaking her 50-ton purse.

"Damn right, you're paying for dry cleaning!"

Her friends grabbed her arm and led her off before she could let fly again.

Flexing my jaw to make sure it was still attached, I stood up. Making my way to the restroom, and avoiding Matt the men's room mutant, I examined the rapidly forming bruise on my face.

I looked like utter hell and it was still an hour until midnight. Guess I was not getting laid tonight.

I threw back a couple of shots at the bar but no longer feeling in the mood to celebrate.

Screw it! I was outa there!

The street outside The Garage was quiet as I made my way to my car.

"Hey, Buddy. Got a dollar to help a guy get a bite?" said a bum as I walked by.

Why not? At least someone could have a Happy New Year. Reaching for my wallet, I knew there was only a five and a ten in there anyway.

It was after I got out my wallet that I saw the baseball bat.

Not again -

WHAM!

Stars circled, and I saw the pretty lights as I fell against a car.

The kicks started coming fast and hard.

"Fucking faggots! Think you're so high and mighty! Goddamn Cocksuckers!"

Each sentence drew another kick. I saw the bat start to raise again and tried to scramble away but my feet would not work right.

Backing in terror, I bumped into someone. Dripping blood, I realized I was looking at white chiffon. Following the leg upward, I realized I was staring up at Pickles McGee.

Shit! Could this get any worse?

Ignoring me, Pickles stepped toward the mugger.

"May I help you, Honey?" she asked.

"This is none of your business, you fucking queen!" roared the mugger.

"Oh, I think it is. You see, this boy and I have unfinished business."

"Fuck off!" Screamed the man as he brandished his bat.

"Wrong answer." quietly answered Pickles.

"I said-" began the mugger but he never got a chance to finish.

BAM! went the purse from hell.

The mugger tried to regain his balance but here it came again.

KWACK!

"Fucking faggot!" screamed the man as Pickles approached him.

"Honey, as you clearly have no idea how to treat a lady, you won't need this."

KERPOW! Those six-inch stilettos hit him right in the groin serving up scrambled eggs on his midnight buffet.

After a muffed "EEP!", the batter was OUT!

Pickles bent over the man.

"Now, that I have your attention, (Groin kick!) let me make one thing clear. (Groin kick!) Ladies need treated with respect. (Groin kick!) Do I make myself clear? (Double groin kick!)"

My rescuer turned and help me up. My face was bleeding, so she handed me a Kleenex.

"Are you okay, Honey?"

"I think so." I mumbled. "I thought you were mad at me."

"I was but I think getting mugged kind of moves the scale in your favor. " she smiled as I staggered against her.

"Besides, " Pickles said as she looked her now blood splattered dress, " someone needs to pay for this dry-cleaning."

She helped me stagger toward the bar.

"What about him?" I gestured toward the passed-out mugger.

"What about him?"

"Should we call the cops?"

"Oh, Honey. The cops aren't gonna do anything to some queerbasher. Besides, he isn't going anywhere." she smiled.

"Why not?" I asked.

"He just doing the same thing everyone is doing on New Year's Eve."

"What's that?"

Pickles smiled fiercely

"Oh, Honey. He's just waiting for his ball to drop!"

And Then It Happened

This is a hard story to tell and one I have put off. An evening with my godson gave me the love and energy to tell it.

****

And then it happened.

I had been out of town for a while and just wanted to relax so I went out to The Garage, of course.

I think it was a Tuesday and for some reason the place was better lit than normal and the crowd was kinda sparse. And to be honest, kinda well-worn.

Don't get me wrong. Everybody has a bad day now and then, but this crowd looked like they had been through the wringer and were ready to DRINK.

I grabbed a beer and looked for a place to sit when I saw Theodore, Larry's boyfriend sitting all by himself at the end of the bar. I went over to say hello and he waived me to a stool beside of him.

We drank in silence for a few minutes as he seemed to struggle with something. Finally, he spoke.

"So, Mike. Have you heard from Larry lately?"

"It's been a few days. I have been down in southern Ohio training for my new job."

Yes, I had been laid off again. The Reagan Recession was great if you were rich but those of us on the bottom rungs of the ladder just kept starting over.

"Yeah, I heard about that. Restaurant manager, right? Bob Evans Farms Restaurants?"

"You got it. ' Down on the Farm'. Yeehaw!" I said tiredly.

"I just can't see you pushing biscuits and gravy." Theodore said.

"Neither could I. BUT, bills are bills."

"Ain't that the truth." he stated as he signaled for another drink.

We drank in silence for a few minutes.

"So, what has Larry been telling you?" he looked at me sideways.

"About?"

"Him?"

I was confused.

"What do you mean? What is going on?" I asked.

"Has he told you what has been happening to him?" asked Theodore as he turned to me.

"Nothing. Why? What is going on?" I shrugged.

"There have been some rumors flying this week."

"Rumors?"

Theodore turned to stare me straight in the eye.

"Rumor has it that Larry has AIDS and was in the hospital this week."

The Earth cracked beneath me and my heart fell into it.

"What do you mean rumors? Aren't you two dating?" I asked.

"He says he has things going on and doesn't have the time to see me right now." he said.

"Doesn't he have a show opening this week?"

"He did but his assistant is running this one."

"Why?" I asked.

"You tell me."

"Have you just asked him?"

"He is avoiding all my calls." Theodore threw me a look. "And his roommate says he isn't home."

"Maybe he's just busy." I hazarded.

"I tried calling at three A.M.!" He sighed. "You know what this means, don't you?"

"What does it mean?"

Theodore threw back his drink.

"If Larry has it, where do you think he got it from?"

"Where?"

Theodore pointed at himself.

"What?" I said.

"If Larry has it, he must have gotten it from me." he said.

"You don't know that."

He sighed.

"Yes, I do. I just got tested."

In that moment, I can honestly say that I wanted to kill him. I wanted to rend him limb from limb and tear the pieces into bits too small to see. I wanted to erase him from existence. I could feel the rage and hatred building up inside me and I wanted to strangle him until his goddamn head popped!

In a boiling rage and a panic that I couldn't control it, I fled the bar.

FUCKFUCKFUCKFUCKFUCKFUCKFUCKFUCKFUUUUUUUUUUUUUUUUUUUCK!

Not Larry!

God, please not Larry!!!

I sat down in my apartment with the phone in front of me.

The answering machine picked up.

"Hey, Larr. It's me. Give me a call." I tried to sound nonchalant.

Two hours later, I call again.

"Hey, Larr, It's me. Mike. Call me when you get the chance."

One hour later.

"Hello, Larry. It's Mike. I need to ask you something."

Thirty minutes later.

"Larry, It's Mike. Call me."

Fifteen minutes later.

"Larry, call me."

Ten minutes later.

"Hey, call me."

Five minutes later.

"It's me."

Suddenly, the phone picked up.

"Micheal, are you drunk?" Larry's deep voice answered.

"Larry, thank God. I need to talk to you."

"What on earth is going on, Micheal?"

"Larry," I began, "I don't know how to ask this, so I am just going to."

"Ask what?" I heard the trepidation in his voice.

"Larry, I have heard a rumor that you have AIDS."

"From who?"

"It doesn't matter. I just need you to tell me right now that you do not have AIDS." I rushed out.

Long pause.

"Larry?"

"Micheal, I'm afraid that I can't tell you that." he said softly.

When those moments hit, you expect to say something significant. I did not.

"Oh." What else was there to say?

"Is that all you have to say. Just 'Oh.'?" asked Larry.

Where are the words?

"Larry, you're my friend and I love you. I'll always be here for you."

A tired sigh came across the line.

"Micheal, you're an idiot." Sigh. "Don't ever change."

Calling Florence Fricking Nightingale

No, I am not a hypochondriac.

I just tend to overreact a little bit when sick.

That little cough could be TB. You know?

That little fever could be bubonic plague. Seriously.

At the first sign of anything, I run to the pharmacy for supplies. The couch becomes a hospital bed and I hole up wrapped in blankets and quilts. Constant pots of tea alternate with fresh boxes of Kleenex to wipe up the drivel. No mummy is better swathed than I.

But, conversely, I tend to think other people react the same way.

Which leads me to knocking on Larry's door about 9 P.M. a couple of days after he told me he had been in the hospital:

"Micheal, what are you doing here?" he asked as he opened the door.

"Well, I got off work about an hour ago, and came to see how you're doing?"

"And what are those?" he said waving towards the five enormous plastic bags I was carrying.

"I thought you might need some supplies."

With a tired sigh, he closed the door behind him and sat down on the porch swing. I heard a burst of laughter come out of the house and realized he had company.

"I'm sorry. I didn't mean to interrupt. I will just leave these here." I moved to set down the bags.

"What is in all of those?" asked Larry.

Well, when I get sick, I like having certain things to help and something always seems to be missing so I brought you extra just in case."

I started to pull things out of the bags. Larry watched in fascination.

"Micheal, I have aspirin."

"Yeah, but these are EXTRA strength."

"Okayyyyy."

"Heating pad." I continued as I pulled items out of the bag. "Vitamins. Cranberry juice."

"Cranberry juice?" he asked.

"I heard it helps you pee."

"THAT has not been a problem, Micheal."

"Just in case." I answered a little uncomfortably.

"What else did you bring?"

"Let's see. Twizzlers. V-8 Juice. Preparation H."

"Preparation H? Micheal, I can assure you that hemorrhoids are not currently a problem." Larry reassured as he started to go through one of the bags.

"I may have overbought a little."

"What is this?" he exclaimed as he held up a famous blue box.

"I don't remember buying those, but I was in a bit of a hurry."

"But Tampax? I don't recall having missed my period."

"I said I was in a rush." I said embarrassed.

Larry sighed.

"Micheal, I am glad you are concerned. -"

"But -" he waived me quiet.

"However, I am fine. Do you hear me? The doctor has even said I can return to work on Monday."

"Oh?"

"Yes, so I am fine." He hugged me, and we sat there eating Twizzlers for a few minutes.

Then, he lightly smacked me upside the head.

"Tampax?!? What were you thinking?" and he laughed.

Christmas In A Leather Bar

I love Christmas, but it has always been a bit problematic for me.

I love to celebrate but I come from a blended family. To make sure we can all meet our obligations, we have met on Christmas Eve for the last quarter century. Once we are done with family obligations, everyone goes their separate ways.

Which leaves the gay guy alone on Christmas.

Again.

Even when I have a boyfriend (or now husband), they also have family obligations frequently leaving me alone on Christmas Day.

Christmas 1987 was no exception. My family had a great time like usual but eventually it came time for me to leave as everyone went off to their "other" families. I climbed into bed and watched holiday movies until I fell asleep.

Christmas Day was beautiful and I was bored silly. You can only pet the cat so much.

Everything was closed except for the gas station on the corner and they got tired of seeing me as I bought them out of eggs and sugar. 30 dozen sugar cookies later I ran out of flour.

Even the snowy weather dampened the noise and limited my travel. Crossword puzzles led to bad poetry led to playing chess with myself. And losing.

Once dark came, my boredom became too much to bear and I had to get out of the apartment before I went buggy. Bundling up like Nanook of the North, I headed out in search of adventure.

Unfortunately, my options were limited by the holiday. Nothing was open. Every restaurant was closed except for a Chinese buffet and there is only so much mayhem you can get up to among the potstickers and Crab Rangoon. Yeehaw!

Which is how I came to be at the Eagle. It was the only place open.

The Eagle was the "leather" bar for Columbus. When I heard about it, a shiver went down my spine that first time as I could only imagine the seedy activities that lay within. Images of hot men in skimpy leather outfits danced in my head like sugar plums.

The reality was quite different. Simply put, it was exactly like all of the other bars except cleaner. Were leather bars supposed have large dance floors with pounding disco music? Most of the clientele didn't even wear leather other than their shoes. How disappointing.

The only "leather" feature that the bar had was a large wooden X, a St. Andrew's cross, leaning against one wall with shackles for both wrists and ankles. I had never actually seen it in use on any of my visits there. Otherwise, the place was pretty white bread.

As it was the only bar open, there was quite an eclectic crowd there that Christmas night. Parkas competed with leather chaps for bar space. The

DJ was trying to raise some dance fever by playing old disco, but no one even managed a few steps.

The only real concession to the holiday was a mannequin made up to look like the Grinch strapped onto the St. Andrew's cross like some hedonistic Santa

Pulling myself up the bar, I ordered a beer and started talking to Bobby, the barback. He was only about 22 and dressed in his normal t-shirt, leather vest, jock strap and assless chaps. Bobby was always good for a joke but that night he appeared a little down.

"What's wrong?" I asked.

"Well, for starters, I am working Christmas night, and no one is tipping." he answered.

"Must be tapped out from holiday shopping. Why else?"

"I was supposed to go to a Christmas party but can't."

"Where?"

"My ex's house." said Bobby.

"Your ex? I thought you hated him."

"I do but who wants to be alone on Christmas?"

"Can't argue with that." raising my beer in agreement I toasted him.

About this time, the DJ gave up and closed down the dance floor. No one talked as they sat and contemplated their drinks. Silence moved in and took hold.

"Screw this!" said Bobby. Climbing up a bar stool, he stepped onto the bar.

And sang.

"Oh, Holy Night, the Stars are brightly shining.

It is the night of our dear Savior's birth!"

His clear tenor rang out through the bar. Heads began to turn.

"Long lay the world in sin and error pining

'Til He appeared and the soul felt its worth"

There is something so pure and simple about a single voice and that song.

"A thrill of hope the weary world rejoices

For yonder breaks a new and glorious morn!"

As the chorus began, other voices started to join in. We all knew every word.

"Fall on your knees

O hear the angel voices

O night divine

O night when Christ was born

O night divine

O night, O night divine"

By the time the first chorus was done, every single man in the bar was singing along.

Looking around I knew why. We were all of the good kids. The chorus boys. The "choir queers". And we all were alone.

By the time the end of the song came around, we all hit that last high "*DiiiiiivIIIIIIINE*" together. I could swear I saw a few guys grabbing their crotches so that they could hit the note.

We spent the rest of the evening singing the Christmas carols we all knew from growing up. There is something almost subversive about a bar full of gay men singing "Silent Night" and knowing every word including the German version. We did that one twice.

"White Christmas" rounded up the evening.

It was wonderful.

I Read The News Today, Oh Boy!

I read the news today, Oh Boy!

Sometimes the events today make me forget what I intended to write and to go off on a completely different tangent.

The headline on Fox News has me quoting the Beatles.

"Gay Couples Marry in Miami-Dade County."

MWAHAHAHAHAHAHAHA!

It has me thinking about the time I was "arrested" because of Miami-Dade County! Truly!

Or should I say because of Anita Bryant. You remember her, right? Former Miss America? Former Country sweetheart? Orange juice spokeswoman?

How about incredibly vicious, antigay bigot?

In case anyone has forgotten, in 1977, Miami-Dade County passed a resolution outlawing housing discrimination against gays and lesbians. That's all. Just said we could live where we wanted to.

That is when Anita Bryant raised her overly teased bouffant and declared that she would not put up with a bunch of "sick perverts cavorting" in a state that she didn't even live in. The words she used were disturbing and insulting and so ill-informed.

To quoth the immortal Anita:

"Practicing homosexuals"

I have never understood that term. I gave up practicing a long time ago. I think I'm pretty good at it by now.

"Bestiality"

I think she got that one wrong. I mean I love animals. I just don't LOOOOOVE animals.

"Pedophiles"

I honestly thought this was for people who had a bicycle fetish. When I found out what it really meant, it convinced me who was really the sick one.

Anita Bryant - that's who!

Seriously, who could even imagine that? Sick. SICK. SICK!

Which is how I came to be standing with a sign screaming on the lawn of the Ohio State House in Columbus.

Anita Bryant had brought her "Save Our Children" codswallop to my hometown for a rally on the State House lawn. Hundreds of her dupes had been assembled and swooned over her every hate filled word. When they could hear her. Which wasn't often.

Anita baby had a little problem with her sound system. It wasn't powerful enough. It was drowned out by the hundreds of boomboxes blaring disco music and the protesters chanting. Loudly!

Poor little Anita couldn't make herself heard past the first rows. Her hate-filled diatribes just got shoved back down her throat on a wave of rainbow colored love.

And that is where it would have stayed if it wasn't for the pie. As Anita tried to make her way through the crowd, a man leaped in front of her with a cream pie and lovingly glazed that bouffant of hers.

And then all hell broke loose. People running. Cops yelling. Poor Anita baby crying. Mayhem reigned.

She never did get to finish her speech.

Which is how I ended up in a paddy wagon with about a dozen other protesters. It was smaller than I thought, and it was quite crowded. Add to that a rather cute Hispanic cop stuck in with us and it was a bit stuffy in there.

SHIT! I was a good kid. I had never been arrested in my life.

As the van started to move, the only thought running through my head was "Oh, my god! What am I going to tell my Dad?"

That is when the paddy wagon turned a corner and stopped. I blinked as the side door opened and the cute cop said, "Come on, ladies. Time to rise and shine!"

Stepping out, I realized that we were in an alley about six blocks from the State House by the Leveque Tower. The cop quickly removed our handcuffs.

Winking at me, the officer said, "Just promise me you have all learned your lesson? Now, get lost!"

And we did. But, I got his number!

So, to refrain, today's headline states that same sex couples are getting married in Miami-Dade County, ground zero for antigay rights.

FUCK YOU, ANITA BRYANT!!!

I Hate "Steel Magnolias"

I had some minor surgery last week and am on some really banging painkillers, so my inhibitions are all gone. Therefore, I am going to reveal a deep personal secret:

I hate "Steel Magnolias".

Truly.

Deeply.

Don't get me wrong. I love "Steel Magnolias".

But, I hate "Steel Magnolias"

Now, before my inbox overflows and my cell phone starts buzzing with outraged queens, let me explain. ("Yes, I am sure you are the head of the International Julia Roberts Fan Club, but for God's Sake take a pill, already!")

Maybe I should retitle this chapter as "Rule No. 1: No Queen Ever Gets To Watch Steel Magnolias Before Attending A Funeral"?

You know why I hate "Steel Magnolias"?

Because I have lived "Steel Magnolias", that's why! You know that scene near the end? YEAH! That one!

It was a windy October day and St. Joseph's Cemetery was as gray as the season. The few leaves remaining on the trees rustled as the minister completed the service. Father Tim was a good man.

The five of us stood there shivering in the wind and watching as the family said their goodbyes and headed to the limos. Finally, it was just us. Beth and I stood holding hands.

"I heard they are going to defrock him for this." said Robert.

"Why?" asked Larry.

"Turns out that you aren't allowed to give a Catholic burial to an unrepentant gay man."

"So, they are going to kick him out of the Church for that?" I chimed in.

"Yep. Bastards!"

After that we all started to move. Everyone except for Carl. I signaled to the others to wait.

"Carl, you okay?"

He looked up at me with a face that was raw and gray. I could tell he was trying to say something, but it wouldn't come out. As the others crowded around him, Carl looked like he couldn't breathe.

"Why?" he finally choked out.

"What?" I asked.

"Why?" he yelled out as he waived his hands towards the casket.

"Honey, it's okay-" Beth started to put her arm on his shoulder.

Carl turned a wide-eyed stare at Beth and shook off her arm and he was OFF!

"WHHHHHYYYYYYY????" came floating across the cemetery.

Running like fools we chased him over grave and tombstone. I am glad that we were the only ones in the place as I am sure we would have been mistaken for psych ward escapees. Shouts of "Carl?" echoed around the field as we tried to catch up with him.

Missing my footing, I tripped over the edge of an open grave and fell in. I could not get out until Robert came along to pull me out.

Clambering up out of the grave, I noticed the others had rounded up Carl.

"You are an idiot!" I snarled.

Carl looked me up from top to bottom. Dirty shoes to muddy hair to the (now) brown tie that Robert had used to haul me up out of the hole.

And he laughed.

"You-" I started.

"Let him laugh." said Larry.

I looked down at myself and then, you know, I laughed too. We all did.

"Laughter through tears is my favorite emotion." quoted Robert.

Shaking our heads, we walked out of the cemetery.

"What now?" asked Carl

I had the best answer.

"I need a drink."

A Little Addiction is a Wonderful Thing

There are many types of addictions

Some people do drugs. Others can't pass a bottle of alcohol on the street without stopping.

I even know people who claim they are addicted to books! I gave up that happy train of thought after my husband made me watch an episode of "Hoarders" on the Discovery Channel. I had nightmares for days.

My addiction is a little different. And my friends had gotten a little worried. They were all waiting for me as I got home from work. Beth, Robert, Larry, a few others were sitting in my living room waiting on me along with my roommate, William.

"Hello? Is this some surprise party I didn't know about? If so, my birthday is in April."

"That is not why we are here." said Robert.

"Then why?"

"Michael, this is an intervention." said Beth.

"Intervention?"

"For people with an addiction." she continued.

"Me? An addict? You have got to be kidding me."

"So....You got arrested again?" asked Larry as he slid onto the stool beside me.

"Sort of..."

He threw me a look.

"Sort of?"

"Kind of..."

"Kind of? Sort of?" Larry sighed. "Were you arrested or not?"

"That would be a yes?" I answered hesitantly.

"Were you charged?"

"Noooooooo...."

"Why not?" he asked.

"Well..."

"You slept with another cop, didn't you?"

"That depends on your definition of 'slept with'." I answered with a huge smile.

"That would be a yes." sighed Larry as he signaled to Beth.

Beth stood and opened a folder. Orange cards fell out.

"Perhaps you could explain these." she asked.

"Notes?"

"Micheal, you know as well as I do that these are warnings for traffic violations."

"I have been stopped a few times..." I shrugged.

"Oh, Honey. This is more than a few times. There are 37 notices here."

Beth grabbed one. "55 miles an hour in a school zone. 55!"

"I was in a hurry."

"Or this one, driving without lights through Riverfront Park. Without lights! You could have killed someone!"

"But I didn't!"

"Why were you taking such a chance?" she demanded.

"Well...."

"I will tell you why! Every single one of these has the police officer's name and phone number on it. Thirty-seven cops!"

"Ummm-" I began.

"And then there are these!" said Jose as he and his hub hauled out a familiar box and dumped it on the floor. Out poured a mound of police caps, nightsticks, and handcuffs. "Fetishes are one thing, young man, but this is a bit much. Did you sleep with all of them?"

"Maybe..."

My roommate William bent down and picked up a sash.

"Micheal, I could forgive you for all but this one. This is a sign of a real problem."

It read "School Crossing Guard".

I felt Larry put his arm around me.

"Do you see why we are worried?" he asked.

"Maybe."

"One of these days, you are actually going to be arrested. You will go to jail and cannot sleep your way out of it. Promise us you will stop it with the police trawling."

"But-"

"Promise now!"

Sigh.

"I promise. Cross my heart and hope to die." I crossed my heart with my fingers and looked at them all.

Taking a breath, they all smiled.

"Let's go get a beer!" I suggested.

"I'm driving!" said Larry.

The Walls Have Ears

The thin walls in my living room have sparked this week's chapter.

Don't you just love it when you hear yourself discussed by other people?

I can be petty, bitchy, and a complete bastard at times...and so are my friends. That is why I love them.

The 80's were no different.

Imagine primping in the mirror for an hour. Yes, to see me now you wouldn't believe it, but I had caught the hair gelling, tight-jeaned bug and was getting ready for a night on the town. I had searched my (admittedly) meager closet and had come up with the outfit of the night.

Mullet haircut?

Check.

Silk shirt?

Check.

Gold chain? (Admittedly, gold-plated but who knew, right?)

Check.

Damn! I looked good.

A spritz of Aramis and I was out the door.

The Garage was hopping that night and I walked in the door like I owned the place. Those queens better get a look at this boy. Yeah, that's right. I have arrived.

Nodding to Pickles, I made my way through the bar and found a place at the bar. There were quite a few cute guys running around but no one I knew. Hmmm, maybe I was going to go home alone.

That is when I saw him. Dark-haired, kinda cute and he was looking at me from an alcove near the end of the bar.

Walking over, I introduced myself.

"Danny." he said shaking my hand. He and his friends were sitting around a small table drinking and watching everyone. Oddly, they were all dressed alike.

"Why are you all dressed in white?"

"This is the Crystal Light Dancers look. Don't you recognize it?" His friends were aghast.

If by Crystal Light Dancers, they meant completely dressed in white, maybe. Or the teased mullets reminiscent of poodles at the Westminster Dog Show, maybe. And enormous mustaches that would have put Freddie Mercury to shame? Maybe.

And they were reviewing everyone for the Red Carpet at the Oscars.

"Did you see those shoes?" asked Danny

"Oh, no. What a disaster?" said Friend Number One.

"Who wears blue jeans with riding boots?" continued Friend Number Two.

"I Know!" said Danny.

And so it went. They started going so fast and furious that it was getting hard to say which of the clones said what.

"White, after Labor Day?"

"How depressing. And that jacket?"

"Ralph Lauren is spinning in his grave."

"Umm." I interjected.

They looked at me as though a potted plant had begun to speak.

"Ralph Lauren's still alive, isn't he?"

Nonplussed, they huffed and continued their prattle. Finally, bored off my ass, I asked if I could get them refills on their drinks and made my way to the bar about ten feet away

You know, acoustics can be a bitch.

After placing the order (three cranberry vodkas), I leaned against the bar to wait. That is when I realized that sound carries really well when the people speaking are in an alcove that is amplifying every sound.

"Oh, my god, Danny. Get rid of him!" said Thing One.

"What a fashion nightmare!" said Thing Two.

"I know! Right?!?" continued Danny.

I began to blush as I listened and watched the bartender make the drinks.

"Who wears Aramis these days?" whispered Danny.

"That is so yesterday!" gabbled Clone Two.

I had, as a matter of fact, bought the cologne the prior day.

"Hasn't he ever heard of Stetson?" kvetched Clone Three.

The bartender was a little slow which allowed me to become more and more humiliated.

"And those shoes!"

"Who wears Adidas these days?"

"Nike is soooo much better, right?!?"

"At least we are getting a free drink out of it." said Danny.

"Right."

"Thank God."

That did it.

Grabbing the tray from the bartender, I began to weave my way back to the table to the snow-white trio.

That is when it happened.

I could swear the shoestring from my cheap ass shoes must have come undone because I tripped and the drinks went flying. The glasses hit the table and bounced splattering the virginal trio with cranberry juice.

Shrieks of outrage began. Those poor puppies looked as though they had walked out of a slasher movie.

"This is silk, you moron." shouted Danny.

"But at least the drinks were free." I smirked and walked off.

The rest of my night had nowhere else to go but up.

My Knight In Shining Armor

or The Complete, Unedited, and Totally True Story of Floyd the Pig

This is a bittersweet tale, but I think that you will like it.

Some of you may think you know this story but you do not know it all, or at least you do not know the whole story and the context in which it occurred. Many of you have heard parts of it but none of you know the whole story. I have changed some of the names to protect privacy.

This is the tale of how a group of people in funny clothing saved my life.

Please grant me this one favor: if you start to read this, please read it through to the final end. This story is important to me and is a bit difficult to tell and it will not go where you expect.

Thank you, Zyggie, for asking the right questions last week and making me tell the story.

Prologue:

I have seen the shadows in a desert night.

I have walked the corridors of abandoned buildings.

The landscape of the Apocalypse is dire and wrapped in smiles and pain.

By the late 1980's, the drumbeats were constant. They came at you from every side.

TV.

Radio.

Newspapers.

Phone.

AIDS.

AIDS.

AIDS.

And on and on.

Walter Cronkite calmly read the numbers on the nightly news. 10,000. 15,000. 20,000. The spiral went up and up.

"The Federal Government has warned that those who engage in high risk activity…"

"Gay men and intravenous drug users are at special risk…"

"Hemophiliacs and children requiring blood transfusions are being affected in unprecedented numbers…"

Drip.

Drip.

Drip.

It was a constant pounding.

I began to fear answering the telephone. Each week the answering machine contained a new one.

"Jimmy died last night."

"I had to take Al to the hospital."

"The funeral is Friday."

Drip.

Drip.

Drip.

At work, it was the same.

"No, you can't get AIDS from a bathroom door handle."

"She looks awful. I bet she has AIDS."

"Betty lost her son - you know, the fag. AIDS."

Drip.

Drip.

Drip.

As every drop hit my psyche, a hammer pounded it into my skull.

I felt as though I were drowning. Every ounce of strength that I had was being taken to keep my own grip on reality let alone being there for others.

I know what it means to go insane as I was staring at the Mountains of Madness.

Drip.

Drip.

Drip.

I even tried a therapist to try to deal but he had to keep rescheduling and rescheduling as he got more and more AIDS patients. Finally, he suggested I look elsewhere.

I could have fought a person. I could have fought an animal but how the hell do you something that is a concept? Something that has no body. Something that is stalking you in the shadows but refuses to come out and goddamn fight!

AAAAAAAAAAAAAAIIIIIIIIIIIIIIIIIGGGGGGGGGGGGGGGGGGGGHHHHHHHHHHHHH!!!!!!!!!!!

My batteries were dying and so was I.

They say it is always darkest before the dawn.

Enter Floyd, Part I

In an effort to make something out of my life, I had enrolled in grad school.

After class, I would hang out in the student union and had fallen in with the science fiction geeks. Big surprise there, right?

Anyway, a bunch of them were talking about some medieval thing coming up that they were all going to.

Did I want to go?

"What is this group called again?"

"Middle Ages, Inc."

"Is this like Monty Python?"

"Uh, no. We really hit people. You have to know about them"

I did not know but had the weekend off and had to do something or I would sit at home and get more and more depressed.

"Hey, Mike. You're a restaurant manager. You okay with making dinner if we bring the supplies?"

"Sure."

Little did I know.

So that is how I ended up in a string tie and work clothes in a forest in West Virginia.

Upon arrival, my friends had determined that there were a few problems with the menu for the event and the facilities.

First, the menu for the feast was unique to say the least. The cook's idea of proper medieval food was pressed turkey rolls, stuffed with cranberries and sour cream, and topped with American cheese.

That is where the second problem came up. No one had checked that the utilities were turned on at the site – and they weren't. So, the pressed turkey rolls were served …cold.

Add to this the fact that it had been raining for the entire prior week and the temperature onsite was a balmy 55 degrees and you have the idea.

I had expected to be asked to make burgers and some brats and maybe some mac and cheese. That's not quite how it turned out.

Upon my arrival, I had been presented with a 60 lb. suckling pig, a bag of apples, a bag of pears, and a double hibachi.

Seriously?

The only whole animal I had ever cooked was a chicken! At the restaurant, the only pork we served was ground!

All other thoughts flew out of my head as the fact that I had people to cook for filled my noggin from stem to stern.

I am nothing if not a cook.

I had a purpose.

Wading into the battle, there were a couple of issues. First and foremost was the fact that the pig was approximately 30 inches long and the skewers I had been given to spit it with were about 24 inches long. So, before I knew it, my hand was somewhere up a pig I never thought it would be wiring two spits together to hold the pig for cooking.

Second issue: While I could certainly stuff the pig with apples and pears, we had no way of sewing it up. I didn't know that you are supposed to bring very long needles and catgut to sew it up and didn't have them if I did.

So, we came up with a unique solution. Kite string. About 300 feet of it. We just kept turning and turning. That poor thing looked like something out of "Charlotte's Web", but it worked. Then we coated it with honey and spices and popped it on the hibachi and prayed for the best.

That is when the third issue cropped up. What comes out of a pig when you are cooking it?

Grease!

Riiiiiiight!!!

Every so often, grease would pour out of the pig and into the hibachi. Flames would shoot up WHOOOSHing up higher than my head. We would pick up the pig, carry it about ten feet away, put it out, wait for the flames to die down and put it back.

"Meltdown!!!" we would scream each time and grab the pig. The tree above us was wilting and we were taking bets on when the eyes would pop.

I won.

Then, we had our final issue. As we were cooking this juicy pig full of fruit and roasting away, another chemical reaction was occurring. Something was building up inside of the pig.

Right!

STEAM!

Imagine our surprise when the kite string began to burn through and pieces of jet powered fruit began popping out of the pig.

Pop!

Wha?

POP!

DIVE!!!!

POP! POP! POP! POP!

We huddled on the ground behind a picnic table while the porcine wonder continued to expel fruit at escape velocity. I swear it looked like the scene from the movie "Alien" where the creature explodes out of the guy's stomach.

Finally, the noises died down and the pig cooked merrily away.

Not having known better, we had placed an apple in its mouth before cooking and that poor apple had been through hell.

After about three hours of blazing atomic fireball, we decided that the porker was done. Both eyes had popped, and we had burned off an ear, but it was done. It was a charred mass of pig.

We laid it out on a platter to cool and that is when I saw the loose string sticking out of the charred mass. Pulling on it, the crust began to peel away until it just slid away revealing the most beautiful looking pig ever. It was truly beautiful despite the fact that the eyes had popped, and we had burned off an ear.

The cremated apple had stuck to the teeth and could not be dislodged so someone got the great idea to fix it up. Grabbing some nail polish, they painted it bright red.

Carrying it onto the hall, my friends all sat down at the table to eat while the whole room stared at the pig. Then at the pressed turkey rolls on their plates. Then back at the pig.

The cook took one look at the pig and disappeared. I never saw him again. There was just one light working in the room and that was directly in front of the "Prince". Staring at his plate, he came to a decision. Picking up his plate, he wandered out of the light. We heard a thump as a plate emptied into the garbage.

Then, he appeared out of the dark at the edge of our table.

"Please, Sir. May I have some more?"

We fed the whole event from that pig.

Floyd the Pig, Part II

Later that same night.

It kept raining the whole day and night. Everyone at the event had either hidden somewhere to drink or were trying to keep warm in their tents.

Guess what I did?

RIGHT!

I was drunk off my ass sitting in a shelter house talking to a friend trying to stay warm and basically babbling. We were so drunk that we were holding each other on the bench to keep from falling off.

The night was dripping along when DJ appeared. DJ was a tall, cadaverous looking, blond man dressed all in black. He had missed dinner and was hungry.

The platter containing the remains of the pig was on a table behind us. What is left of a pig once you are done eating. A few bones...the tail...and what else? The head.

We heard DJ fiddling with the platter but were honestly too drunk to pay too much attention. Until -

"My, what a handsome pig you are."

Wha?

We carefully turned around so as not to draw attention to ourselves. DJ has picked up the pig head and was doing his best Hamlet and Yorick imitation. We quickly turned back around before he noticed.

"My, what a sexy pig you are!"

Turning back around, we noticed him staring eye to eye with the pig head. Titillated but slightly terrified, we quickly swiveled back away before he saw.

"My, what a sensuous pig you are!"

That did it. No longer caring and too drunk not to watch, we swiveled around and planted our feet to keep from falling off.

DJ had picked up the pig head and was playing with it. He has forced his hand up the neck of the pig into where its brain had used to be before I had boiled it away. His thumb went below the tongue of the beast and he began to do ventriloquism with it.

That is how Floyd the Pig was born.

Popping the jaw, he began to talk to the pig head.

"Hi! Would you like to meet my friend, Floyd?"

Who could resist?

Now that Floyd was his best friend, DJ began to make the rounds of the camp to introduce everyone.

Imagine a tall gentleman in a cloak steps out of the dark.

"Hi! Would you like to meet my friend, Floyd?" and he would appear from under the cloak.

We traced him all around the camp by the screams.

Finally, deciding that Floyd was now his best friend, and having introduced him to everyone in the woods, DJ decided that the pig head deserved a night on the town. Hopping on his motorcycle, he started up and got ready to go.

There was, however, a problem. He only had one helmet so guess who got it? Right! FLOYD! And he was off into the night!

We later found out he had grabbed someone else's helmet and it didn't even belong to him.

DJ and Floyd hit the hottest night spots in Huntington, West Virginia that night, and DJ paid the cover charge for the pig head! All I can envision is a pig head rising above the dancers going "Staying Alive! Staying Alive!".

As Floyd was now his best friend, DJ was determined to keep him around as long as he could. If your best friend was a pig head and you wanted to keep him as long as possible, what would you do with him?

You'd put him in the fridge! Right next to the eggs, the butter, the orange juice... and that is what he did and headed to bed.

About six am, DJ's girlfriend came home from work and decided she wanted some orange juice.

He said all he heard was a scream...and then she began to beat him to death with the pig.

Floyd the Pig, Part III

Have you ever had a really champion hangover?

You know the kind I mean, right? The ones where you can hear your eyeballs moving. That was me.

To stay dry, I had put my sleeping bag on a picnic table in a shelter house and had gone to sleep. Consciousness was not my friend.

RRRRRRIIIIIIIIIIPPPPPP!!!

"Te Hee Hee Hee! Te Hee Hee Hee! Quick! He's waking up!"

RRRRRRIIIIIIIIIIPPPPPP!!!

"Te Hee Hee Hee! Te Hee Hee Hee!"

Wha?

RRRRRRIIIIIIIIPPPPP!!!

Maybe I better pay attention to this?

Opening my eyes, they were stabbed by the morning light. PAIN!

"Te Hee Hee Hee! Te Hee Hee Hee!"

RRRRRRIIIIIIIIPPPPP!!!

Lifting my head, I looked down my body and realized that my feet were duct taped within the sleeping bag to the picnic table beneath me. There was another band around my waist. A third band of duct tape was wrapped around my chest and shoulders where they peeked out of the bag.

"Te Hee Hee Hee! Te Hee Hee Hee!"

Turning my head, I saw two ladies standing nearby holding a large roll of duct tape and giggling.

"What is going on?" I groaned out.

"Te Hee Hee Hee! Te Hee Hee Hee! We are going to find out what is under your kilt!"

"Very funny, ladies. Now, please cut me loose."

"Not until we find out what is under that kilt!"

With that, a five-finger glacier came down my boxers and grabbed something no other woman has seen since my mother.

"Aighh!" I shouted and jumped. Or more like skipped as the picnic table moved a few inches as the glacier disappeared.

"We are going to find out what is under your kilt!" and again the glacier returned.

Grab. Arch. Grab. Arch. Eventually, the ladies jumped on top of me to keep the table from moving.

That is when I noticed that everyone at the event was standing around the shelterhouse and watching...but no one was helping!

Eventually, Randy strode up and pulled them off me.

"Girls! Leave that boy alone! If he wanted to sleep with you, he would have done it. Just like everybody else."

With that, he cut me loose.

That is when Randy told probably the only lie in his whole life as he grabbed the band of duct tape around my shoulders.

"If we do this real fast, it won't hurt!"

Epilogue

Several hours later, after the bleeding had stopped and the ladies had apologized, I sat on a bench drinking a beer and mourning my lost chest hair.

Sitting next to me was Bear, one of the furriest men I have ever met. He was sucking on a cigarette and watching me.

That is when it hit me.

"Whoa!" I said.

"What?" asked Bear.

"I just realized I haven't thought about the real world for three straight days." I felt great!

Bear took a long drag on his cigarette.

"Welcome to the Middle Ages!", he said.

The King of Pain

Hearing that one of my favorite authors passed today inspired this story. This is for you, Sir Terry Pratchett:

I have a tattoo.

If you haven't seen it, I have a Pegasus the size of my hand on my left pec. It is the size of a leaf and has red, blue and yellow in it.

Most of my friends have tattoos these days but when I got this one, no one did. It was considered edgy and a bit seedy. Yeah, that's me - edgy. Riiiiiight.

I never know what quite got into me. I woke up on my first day off after six weeks working straight at the restaurant. And something was wrong.

Wait. Hmmmm?

Oh, I didn't have to work!

My body instinctively woke me up at 5 am. I rolled over and tried to go back to sleep. Nope. No such luck.

I turned on the TV...and was bored witless. Nothing on.

I started reading "The Color of Magic" by Terry Pratchett but just found that it made me even more agitated.

All my friends were busy.

Slamming a two liter of Mountain Dew, I was buzzing higher than a kite and ready for anything!

Damn!

By 9 am, I was at my wit's end.

That's when it hit me...

Screw it! I was going to get a tattoo!

That's right, Buckaroo! This boy was going to get a tattoo!

Then the question became where? Tattoo parlors were a lot more highly regulated then and it was difficult to find one.

So, I grabbed the phone book. You remember those, right? Big, thick and yellow?

There were four ads.

"Wild Man's Tattooing and Piercing Emporium" featured a picture of a burning skull riding a Harley.

Um...no.

"Cassie's Pet Shop and Tattoo Parlor" had a cartoon showing a fearsome looking kitten sporting an anchor on his arm.

Reeked of bestiality.

"Tribal Tattoos" featured some really crappy looking artwork consisting mainly of poorly drawn tiki idols.

"Bad Ass Bob's" had some great artwork but also prominently featured the words "clean" and "hygienic".

We had a winner!

Calling I got the hours and found out they were only an hour away. That's right. Unlike today where they are more common than hookers, tattoo parlors were few and far between. No one wanted the stigma associated with "that" sort of place.

It must have been the Mountain Dew, but that hour flew by. Suddenly, there I was!

I don't know what I expected but a brightly lit shop resembling a dentist's office was not it.

But "Bad Ass Bob" certainly was...bad ass, I mean. Tall, bearded and hair down to his waist, he wore biker leathers and a T-shirt marked "Your Pain Is My Gain!".

"Hello?" he rumbled.

"Are you Bob?"

"If you are drunk or high, GET OUT!!!" Bob roared.

"I'm neither." I squeaked out.

"Really?!?" he loomed above. "How old are you, kid?"

"Twenty-Four." I swear my voice cracked.

Bob examined every inch of me over his glasses. Admittedly, I was skinny, well, scrawny was the better word, and the big horn-rimmed glasses didn't help.

"I.D., please."

I handed him my wallet.

"Okay, kid. Are you sure this isn't some frat prank?"

"No, sir. I graduated two years ago."

Bad Ass Bob sighed and said, "Okay....That is $350 upfront. What did you want and where?"

OMHYGOD!

In the rush to get there, I hadn't even thought about what I wanted. It had to go somewhere my shirt would cover because Bob Evans didn't allow their managers to have visible tattoos, but what?

Thousands of tattoos covered the walls.

Screaming skulls...no.

Giant breasted Martian babes...not quite the look I wanted.

Strawberry Shortcake...really!?!

"Do you have any Scooby Doos?" I asked.

"Sorry. Can't do trademarked stuff."

Then, it hit me. Here I am trying to break out of my rut and wanted to fly.

"Do you have any Pegasus?"

Bob looked at me kind of odd.

"Funny you should mention that. I drew up a real nice one last night. Don't know what got into me but here it is." And he pointed.

It really was beautiful. The myth of Bellerophon breaking the bonds of Earth upon the back of Pegasus was always one of my favorite myths. I always wished that could have been me.

Maybe it could.

I was so skinny that he had trouble placing the stencil. Bob didn't want to place the stencil over top of a joint or right on a bone because of the pain involved. My shoulder was out, and my upper arm was so thin that the stencil went all the way around.

My chest it was.

Bob's studio was immaculate, and the tools came straight from the autoclave.

"You know this is a needle, right, kid?"

"As long as I don't look, it will be fine."

"Ooookay."

YEAH, it was a needle all right and it fucking hurt!!!!!

After about five minutes, Bob looked at me and send, "Could you please stop that?"

"Stop what?"

"That sound..."

I thought it was the machine making that high-pitched whine.

"Sorry."

Bob started up again. Five more minutes passed.

"Kid, you sound like a puppy in pain. Are you sure this is okay?"

"Yes, sir."

"Okay."

And, he went to work again.

I guess he couldn't take my whining anymore because he stopped and got up and went into his workroom. Coming back, he handed me a beer.

"For the pain." Bad Ass Bob said.

Four beers and three hours later, it was done.

And it was - and is - beautiful.

Fish Out Of Water

The other day, I lost a friend unexpectedly. When I was new and moving in unfamiliar circles, she took me in and always had my back. This story is for you, Judy.

****

As much as I like to think I have been out of my depth coming out in the gay world at times, that is nothing compared to my friend, Gregory.

I met him at the Garage one night. He was very hard to miss. Tall and broad, it wasn't just the dark coat or the suspenders. Even the large dark hat didn't quite set him apart.

I guess it was the chin beard. Not a VanDyke and not a mustache and beard. Just a chin beard.

He had walked straight off the label of the Quaker Oats box.

Everyone was staring, and he looked like he was about to wilt. He was tucked in a corner table and watching the nightly bar parade go by with wide-eyed wonder.

Everyone at the bar seemed to be a little afraid of him as if his wholesomeness would explode. And the only open bar stool was at the end of the bar next to where he was sitting.

Plopping myself down, I ordered a beer and tried to relax.

The next thing I knew, there was a light touch on my elbow and I found myself eye to eye with this man.

"Pleasant evening to you." he said with a light accent that lilted.

"And you as well. Ummm, you are...?"

"Amish.", he quickly answered back a little nervously.

Well that answered that.

"Nice to meet you, Amish. My name is Mike."

Smiling, he extended his hand and said, "Gregory."

"I have to ask this. You do know you are in a bar, right?"

"Oh, yes."

"And, you do know this is a gay bar, right?" I queried.

"Oh, yes. Even better." he looked around a bit furtively as he spoke.

"Why are you here?"

"For the same reason you are, I would say."

"To meet men?"

"Oh, yes."

"For sex?"

"Oh, yes. Hopefully." he chimed back.

"Are there really gay Amish men?" I asked very naively.

"We prefer the term 'bachelor farmer'." Gregory smiled.

"Hmmm. That makes sense but what are you actually doing here? I thought the Amish shunned modern life and its complications."

"Even we have our teenage wild years. I am on my Rumspringa.", he grinned.

"What is that?"

"The Rumspringa is when young Amish get a chance to go wild and experience the outside world. We get a chance to see what we are missing before we make our formal commitment to the Amish church and are baptized."

"So, you can drink?"

"Yes."

"Use an electric lightbulb."

"Yes."

"Ride in a car?"

"Yes."

"Have sex?"

"Hopefully. And soon at that." he chimed.

"Really?" I asked.

"You up for it?"

"Thank you but no. I didn't think there were gay Amish."

"You would be surprised. The kids are allowed to experience life outside the community and find out about the outside world and then decide if they want to leave or stay." Gregory sighed.

"If you leave?"

"You are shunned. No more contact with family."

"Wow, that's harsh."

"But it can be easier that the alternative."

"Going back?"

"Yes. Imagine trying to tuck yourself into a box that doesn't quite fit. And, knowing that that box is the only existence you will ever have."

"That's harsh."

"Yuuuuup." he tilted his now empty glass at me.

"How did you find out about this place?" I waved my hand.

"I saw an article in a newspaper back in 1980 about the "Gay Bars of Ohio".

"And you remembered?"

"No, I saved it." and he pulled it out of his pocket.

"You saved this article for seven years?"

"Oh, yes. And hid it in my Bible."

"Your Bible?" I asked a bit incredulous.

"Yes, along with articles on farming and the weather and the sandem."

"Sandem?"

"Oh, yes. Here is one." and he handed me a yellowed page from a magazine.

"Um, Gregory. We don't call that sandem."

"You don't?"

"No. Um. We use the term "S and M".

"Oh, okay. I will keep that in my mind."

"Do you know what S and M is?" I asked.

"Oh, yes." he said. "That would be the leather."

Score one for farmboy!

"Where did you get this?"

"Mainly old magazines."

"And have you ever...?"

"Ever what?" he asked.

"Slept with a guy?"

"I'm Amish - not neutered." he shyly smiled.

"How?"

"I would suspect in the usual way.", he smiled.

After that we spent the rest of the evening talking.

I saw Gregory many times that summer and he certainly developed a passion for bright colors. Greens and pinks seemed to be his favorite and I never saw him without a drink in his hand.

I will always remember him in full Amish clothing riding the float for the Eagle during the Gay Pride Parade surrounded by men wearing less clothing than the leather in his boots. And, he was having the time of his life!

Eventually, he met someone nice and I saw them running around town whenever I went out.

Until -

I walked into the Garage and there was Gregory, dressed in all his Amish splendor.

"Gregory, why are you dressed that way?"

"It's time to go home. Time to settle down."

"But what about...um, what was his name?"

"Robert." he sighed.

"Yeah, what about Robert?"

"Robert left me for an air steward for Delta."

"That bastard!"

"He said I was too naive. Maybe he was right." Another sigh.

"So, you are going back?"

"Yes."

"Are you sure?" I asked.

"Oh, yes. I have sown my wild oats and I miss my family."

"But -"

"It is time, Micheal. You have been good to me and I wanted to see you before I went."

"But-"

"It has been wonderful. I will not forget you."

With that he glided out the door and into the night. A few minutes later, I swore I heard the sound of horses moving off.

I never saw him again.

However, I always had hope that he found a "bachelor farmer" of his own.

Happy Birthday, Jungle Boy!

"Whhhhhaaaaaaatttt?!?"

"SHHHHHH! Keep it down! People are staring."

"You're moving where?" asked Larry.

"West Virginia." said I.

"What on earth for?"

"I need a job, Larr."

"And you can't find one somewhere that actually has LIFE?" he asked wide-eyed.

"It's West Virginia! Not the goddamn MOON!"

"It might as well be..."

And...

"Son, you are moving where?"

"West Virginia, Dad."

"Really?" he asked with a raised brow.

"I have to work."

"You know it took us 100 years for the family to get OUT of West Virginia, right?"

"Yup."

"Oh, Son..." my father sighed.

****

That is how I came to be driving through a completely abandoned block in Huntington, West Virginia. Row after row of abandoned buildings and empty lots where buildings used to be. To say it was bleak and foreboding was being mild.

And I was looking for a gay bar out here?

Two months of working every single day made me realize that the only people I knew were my employees. They may have been nice people, but I was the boss and they wanted nothing to do with me once they left work. I was lonely. I was bored.

And it was my birthday...

And, God Damn It, I wanted a beer!

Larry had looked up the address for me of the only gay bar listed for the whole state in the Gay Yellow Pages. There had to be more, but this was the only one listed.

The Driftwood Lounge.

Seventh Avenue and the middle of nowhere. The buildings that still stood didn't have numbers, so I had to make a guess. Parking the car under the only working streetlight for blocks, I started walking down the block looking into abandoned buildings.

Yup. Here was Mr. Big City Urban Gay creeping around like an extra in some bad 80's slasher movie. At any moment, a man in a hockey mask could pop out swinging a chainsaw and chasing me across the land. WHOOOOOOO! AIIIGH!

I almost peed my pants as an honest to god owl sped by. All that we needed to complete the picture was ---

HOooooOOOooooooooWL!

A howling dog.

I was about to turn around and head back when I saw a flash of light about a block ahead as a door opened. Approaching the building, I thought I had made a mistake until I heard it. That thumpa-thumpa-thumpa.

The door opened again, and a song drifted out and I knew I had found it. Either that or some redneck coal miner was playing "I'm Every Woman" by Chaka Khan.

I had never seen so many drag queens in one spot in my life. I had walked in expecting banjos playing from "Deliverance" and instead has walked into "Priscilla, Queen of the Desert". My prejudices were showing.

Sidling up to the bar, I ordered a beer and looked around.

"First time here?" asked the bartender.

"Yeah. I just moved here." I said.

"You moved here? Honey, most people are trying to move away." He extended a hand. "Jimmy Hobbs."

"Did you say Hobbs?" as we shook.

"Yes. That's me." he smiled.

"That's my last name. Mike Hobbs."

"Well, nice to meet you, Dearie."

"You know, my family moved out of West Virginia."

"Then we must be long lost cousins, kiddo." He handed me a shot of whiskey. "Welcome home!

"Are there a lot of gay people here?"

He waved his hands around.

"We are everywhere."

Looking around at the hundred or so people in the bar, I realized that I felt more at home than I had at any time since I had moved.

"Almost Heaven, right?"

"You got it, kiddo. Happy Birthday!"

A Quilt Is Meant To Keep You Warm

I am glad to have introduced my friend, Larry, to you all. It is amazing how many of you have asked what he is doing now.

Just so you know, I talk to him every day.

He is my moral compass after all...

****

The National Mall, Washington, D.C., 1992

It was a beautiful Spring Day and I was walking over the green talking to Larry and enjoying the sun.

I had never been to Washington, D.C. before and was surprised by the size of the National Mall. Marble glistened in the light and the feeling in the air was that of a festival.

We had already run into Robert and he had told me where to find Al near the Lincoln Memorial. Couples wandered by hand in hand and I could swear I heard Donna Summer music wafting over the hill.

Brightly colored fabric lay on the ground and people lay on them talking. Some laughed. Some told stories.

"Where is it?" I asked Larry as we wandered along. The map I had been given was of minimal use and it was luck more than anything when I stumbled across it.

Blue was the predominant color but the fabric lying there also had red, green and yellow splashed across it. It was beautiful.

"They did a nice job." said Larry.

They had.

****

Huntington, WV 1988

The call came through just as the lunch crowd cleared out. Steve, the senior manager, called me to the office and handed me the phone.

"Mike Hobbs, how can I help?"

"Mike, it's Carl."

"Carl? What are you doing calling me here?" I asked while closing the office door to shut out the noise.

"Sorry to call but I just need to know when you are arriving?"

"Arriving? For what?"

Pause

"Shit. Didn't anybody tell you?"

Annoyed, I snapped, "Tell me what?"

Pause.

"Larry died last night."

"What?"

"Larry died last night."

The world went silent around me. Groping for a chair, I huddled around the receiver.

"What happened?"

"Pneumonia. God, I thought you knew."

"No, not at all."

My soul ripped at that moment and innocence ended.

Paradise truly lost.

All the people and sounds became distorted and muted as though hearing them through water. Hanging up, I had to be alone.

Dragging myself to the walk-in cooler, tears came unbidden where no one could see me. Snot poured down and tears ran down my cheeks. Huge wracking sobs poured out.

I felt completely lost.

I have no idea how long I lay there when the door opened. James, the dishwasher, came in and saw me.

"Bad, eh?" he asked through missing teeth.

I could only nod.

"Here. Use this." he handed me a dishtowel. "Be right back."

Grabbing a case of sausage, he disappeared.

Shit!

James was back in a few minutes.

"You don't see this." he said as he pulled a bottle of whisky out from behind the frozen waffles. Taking a swig, he handed it to me. "What happened?"

"Someone died."

"I figured. Parent?"

"Best friend."

"Fuck." James said sliding down next to me among the cases of sausage.

"That sucks."

"Yeah, it does." I said, handing him the bottle.

"How old?"

"28"

"Double fuck." Swallow. "AIDS?"

"How-?"

"I may be a redneck but I ain't blind. No girlfriend and never talk about one neither."

We passed the bottle back and forth. Silence seemed best.

Finally, I made a decision and stood up.

"Mike?" said James from behind me.

"Yeah?"

"You might want to check yourself in a mirror. The staff should never see the manager looking like hell."

That coming from a man that I wasn't even sure could put a sentence together a few minutes earlier.

"Thanks."

****

D.C.

"I like it but why the teddy bear?" I asked.

"I like teddy bears. Besides, when you work with kids…" said Larry with a shrug.

It was officially The Names Project, but most people just called it The AIDS Quilt. Started in 1985, it was a way for people to remember their loved ones. Three by six swatches of fabric covered the landscape in the largest piece of public art ever created. I was told it weighed over 15 tons.

I had expected a lot more sadness. And, there were tears, but that wasn't what you remembered.

The balloons everywhere. The flowers. The laughter floating on the breeze. THAT you remembered. There were even kids running around. The crowds were enormous.

And the MUSIC!

I had expected a funeral and arrived at a picnic.

****

1988

The next morning, I drove the three hours back to Ohio in a daze. The service didn't start until the afternoon and I had no idea what to do with myself. Feeling lost, I went to the only place I knew I could.

Home.

Yeah, home.

Dad knew immediately that something was wrong. I was gray and rumpled and was clearly in distress.

Rosemary gave me some tea, but I couldn't keep up the normal chitchat.

Finally, my Dad said, "Son, what's wrong?"

"Dad, I don't know what to say."

"You can tell us anything."

"I know but I just don't know how to say this."

My father spoke with a note of fear.

"We love you, Son, and you can tell us anything."

Oh, God! They think I have it!

That's when I completely lost it. Fear, love and hurt erupted in one huge burst. Blubbering, I told the story. The pain and the hurt. The fear and the utter feeling of loss.

"It's not me. My friend, Larry, died – "

I couldn't continue. The pain was just too much.

"It's not goddamn fair! Why? Why!?!?"

I couldn't stop crying. No, I didn't want to stop crying. Ever.

"Dad, I am a nobody, but he was someone special. So talented. So---" The pain welled up.

That is when my Dad did the most wonderful thing he has ever done and one I will remember always.

He put his arm around me.

He put his arm around his 25-year-old son and just let me cry. And cry I did. Down to the bottom of my heart. Huge, wracking sobs.

And Dad held me like a child trying to make the hurt go away. And, somehow, the world kept turning.

Somehow...

I love my Dad.

****

D.C.

The sunshine on my face made me smile. It was a beautiful day.

Robert had asked me to meet him by the tidal pool and I was sitting on the edge looking into the water. The breeze made the water ripple and the flags snapped. The Lincoln Memorial stood in the distance.

"Mike?" I turned.

Jose's Dan stood there carrying several large bags.

"What's all that?"

"Well, let's see. Tulips, cause my Jose always loved tulips. And, then, I have his feather boa here."

"Why?"

"It's Jose. That's why."

No other explanation was needed.

"And the third bag?" I asked.

"Lunch, of course." he shrugged.

"Of course."

So, we sat and munched chips and watched the world pass.

"Have you seen Robert? He was supposed to meet me here."

"He must still be over at Al's plot. It is quite crowded over there."

"For Al?"

"No, for Freddy Mercury."

****

1988

I don't remember the service. It makes me sound like a prick but I don't.

All I remember is the numbness. Total top to bottom numbness.

Everybody and everything moved in slow motion.

And then it was over.

We all ended up at a tavern in the Short North for the wake.

All of us sat there in complete silence drinking, sniffling and completely lost.

The jukebox quietly played.

We had reached bottom.

No one even had the strength to ask "Why?".

To fill the silence, someone turned up the jukebox. And, of course, The Beatles started.

"When I find myself in times of trouble, Mother Mary comes to me. Speaking words of wisdom..."

That is when the singing started. I don't know who started it. Probably, Tom, Larry's roommate.

"Let It Be"

It just sort of reached out to us. Familiar and warm. The words were a bit of calm in the dark.

By the time it ended, I was the only one not singing.

I couldn't.

I couldn't!

I hadn't been there!

I hadn't been there when he needed me!

"I HADN'T BEEN THERE!!!" I silently screamed.

That's when it started - "Bohemian Rhapsody".

Then I heard Larry say as plain as day "Micheal, you're an idiot. I'll always be here. Get back to living your life."

And Freddy Mercury sang.

And, then, so did I.

****

D.C.

"Wow! That's amazing." whispered Robert.

And it was.

Freddy Mercury's panel could only be described as beautiful. Hand-beaded velvet and satin. It was also covered with flowers. So many flowers they spilled out on the nearby panels such as Al's.

I went to move the extra flowers and Robert stayed my hand.

"Leave them. Al wouldn't mind."

He was right. Al wouldn't.

Robert and I stood watching people wander by. Finally, it was time to go.

"Where do you want to eat?"

"You decide."

In my head, Larry said, "I am going to go hear Freddy Mercury sing."

"Larry, Freddy Mercury is dead."

"And?" he grinned.

"True."

As we wandered off, Larry said, "Micheal, you're an idiot."

Grin.

"Don't ever change."

THE END

Thanks to the following:

My husband, Jim, for putting up with me all these years.

M. Karen Guth for the cover design.

Teresa Turner for being my "Oldest Friend On The Planet"

And, the 18,000 weekly readers I had while working on this tale.

Thank you for reading my book.

Please note any song lyrics quoted do not belong to me and are the sole property of the copyright owner.

Copyright M.J. Hobbs 2018

Made in the USA
Middletown, DE
17 June 2018